MELLON SQUARE

MELLON SQUARE
Discovering a Modern Masterpiece

Susan M. Rademacher

WITH ESSAYS BY
Charles A. Birnbaum
Patricia M. O'Donnell
Richard C. Bell
and Barry W. Starke

An initiative of The Cultural Landscape Foundation
Charles A. Birnbaum, series editor

Princeton Architectural Press
New York

Modern Landscapes

TRANSITION & TRANSFORMATION

This Cultural Landscape Foundation series focuses on historically important midcentury works that have undergone significant change. Each publication in the series chronicles the planning and design motivations behind the work, illuminates its history, places it within its historical design context, and, perhaps most importantly, draws attention to midcentury landscape treasures while raising awareness of their unique design value, inherent vulnerability, and historic preservation needs. Edited by Charles A. Birnbaum, the foundation's president, the series balances programmatic, design, historic preservation, and environmental concerns while providing a best-practices model. Depending on the landscape, this may include research and documentation efforts, design and treatment interventions, or ongoing management practices and strategies.

Published by
Princeton Architectural Press
37 East Seventh Street
New York, New York 10003

Visit our website at www.papress.com.

Also in this series:
Lawrence Halprin's Skyline Park, by Ann Komara

Editor: Meredith Baber
Designer: Jan Haux

Special thanks to: Sara Bader, Nicola Bednarek Brower, Janet Behning, Megan Carey, Carina Cha, Andrea Chlad, Barbara Darko, Benjamin English, Russell Fernandez, Will Foster, Jan Cigliano Hartman, Mia Johnson, Diane Levinson, Jennifer Lippert, Katharine Myers, Jaime Nelson, Jay Sacher, Rob Shaeffer, Sara Stemen, Marielle Suba, Paul Wagner, Joseph Weston, and Janet Wong of Princeton Architectural Press
—Kevin C. Lippert, publisher

Library of Congress Cataloging-in-Publication Data
Rademacher, Susan M., 1954–
Mellon Square : discovering a modern masterpiece / Susan M. Rademacher with essays by Charles A. Birnbaum, Patricia M. O'Donnell, Richard C. Bell, and Barry W. Starke.—First edition.
pages cm —(Modern landscapes: transitions and transformations)
ISBN 978-1-61689-133-6 (paperback)
1. Mellon Square (Pittsburgh, Pa.) 2. Simonds and Simonds. 3. Mitchell & Ritchey. 4. City planning—Pennsylvania—Pittsburgh. 5. Pittsburgh (Pa.)—Buildings, structures, etc. I. Birnbaum, Charles A., writer of supplementary textual content. II. Title.
NA9072.P59M457 2014
712'.50974886—dc23

© 2015 Princeton Architectural Press
Printed and bound in China
18 17 16 15 4 3 2 1 First edition

2014006802

Contents

Editor's Foreword

Polishing the Jewel

Charles A. Birnbaum, FASLA, FAAR

The second monograph in the Modern Landscapes: Transition and Transformation series is dedicated to Pittsburgh's Mellon Square, built in 1955 and the first Modernist garden plaza in America to be built over a parking garage. Designed by landscape architects John Ormsbee Simonds and Philip Simonds, of Simonds & Simonds, in collaboration with architects James A. Mitchell and Dahlen K. Ritchey, of Mitchell & Ritchey, the plaza was paid for by the Mellon family foundations and conceived as an urban oasis—a public gathering space nested within a cluster of buildings by prominent architects, including Daniel H. Burnham (the Greek Classical Oliver Building) and Harrison & Abramovitz (the Modernist Regional Enterprise Tower, formerly called the Alcoa Building). The plaza was a cornerstone of the Pittsburgh Renaissance, an initiative established by the Pittsburgh Regional Planning Association at the end of World War II to transform the industrial downtown area into a modern city composed of plazas, parks, and new corporate buildings.

 The example of Mellon Square contrasts strongly with the first site in this series, Lawrence Halprin's Skyline Park in downtown Denver, where stewards placed little or no value on its original design, resulting in a disastrous alteration. In contrast, Mellon Square's unique and historically significant design intent and Modernist character have been very well chronicled, documented, and analyzed, which has informed the project work in this book. The result: a renewed, enhanced, and revitalized Mellon Square that carefully balances the highest historic preservation standards with clearly articulated performance benchmarks and sustainability standards.

 Mellon Square is also distinct within a national context. Unlike many other Modernist works of landscape architecture that have met an untimely demise due to decades of deferred maintenance, Pittsburghers have never fallen out of love with Mellon Square, even when it was in a diminished state. I learned this firsthand in 2007 when the Pittsburgh Parks Conservancy invited me to lecture about the iconic plaza in order to energize local business leaders and champions of parks and open spaces. The effort was not difficult, because the local design community valued this nationally significant work. What we discovered at a symposium dedicated to Simonds two years later was how strong and deep of a bond Pittsburghers, as well as landscape architects throughout the country, had with Mellon Square.[1]

Upon reflection today, in preparing for and delivering that initial lecture in 2007, I learned a number of things. First, during Mellon Square's previous renovation in 1989, a then-retired John Simonds was brought back to consult, via his successor firm, Environmental Planning & Design (EP&D). This collaboration differed from other situations where the original landscape architect was never asked to consult (e.g., Lawrence Halprin in Denver, Dan Kiley at Lincoln Center), and suggests that Simonds's design legacy, and the designer himself, was held in high regard (even though we have since learned that Simonds and EP&D weren't in agreement with some of the design changes made at the time).

Second, unlike many other landscape architects of the postwar years, Simonds published extensively throughout his entire career, thus making his design approach and specific design recommendations for Mellon Square clear and accessible. Recognition of Simonds's contributions to the cityscape was boosted by the listing in late 2013 of the Allegheny Commons on the National Register of Historic Places, which included substantial 1960s Simonds & Simonds designs, such as the once-threatened and extraordinary trapezoidal-shaped Lake Elizabeth. The designation is all the more important because, as the city's oldest mapped parkland, the period of significance spanned a century, from 1868 to 1967.

Finally, in a match made in heaven, the adoption of Mellon Square by the Pittsburgh Parks Conservancy (founded in 1996) helps to write a new chapter in the Pittsburgh Renaissance. The Conservancy is the go-to nonprofit partner in restoring and managing public parks. Their efforts, which cannot be understated, are unlike similar regional organizations that were founded around Olmsted-centric networks of parks and boulevards (e.g., Louisville, Buffalo, and Seattle). Here, under the project management of their parks curator (the first such position for a parks organization), the Conservancy broadened its portfolio beyond picturesque and naturalistic neighborhood-based parks to include a downtown site, the Modernist Mellon Square. In 2008, with lead gifts from the Richard King Mellon Foundation and the BNY Mellon, the Conservancy began work on a strategy for renewal. Led by landscape architect Patricia M. O'Donnell of Heritage Landscapes, the square now benefits from a comprehensive strategy for its preservation, restoration, maintenance, and programming.

Now that the jewel has been polished and the Conservancy's curator, Susan M. Rademacher, has told the rich story behind its evolution, will the first Modernist garden plaza built over a parking garage in America achieve the highest honor that can be bestowed on a property in the United States—designation as a National Historic Landmark? Based on the admiration that Pittsburghers feel toward Simonds, one that I would place on the same emotional plane as another creative postwar son, Andy Warhol, I would suggest that it is just a matter of time.

Introduction

An Ascendant Urban Space Restored

Patricia M. O'Donnell, FASLA, AICP

As a product of the city's first renaissance, the Modernist design of Mellon Square was a focal element in reimagining gritty Pittsburgh. Initial research and planning, starting in 2008, afforded the opportunity to study the context from which this intricate jewel of urban design emerged. Positioned over streets and storefronts, the space rose above the hustle and bustle as an oasis. At the same time, it acted as a lens through which to understand the forces of durability and deterioration, and the meanings and daily life of the place.

Gathering a wealth of documentation, observing use, studying context, and investigating details led to analysis of the plaza's initial design and built character. What emerged was a clear picture of the design team's masterful manipulation of urban fabric to revitalize the central business district. Although this was a Mitchell & Ritchey and Simonds & Simonds collaboration, documents pointed to John O. Simonds as the author of sketches that embodied the plaza's design concepts. It was evident that these studies drew on diverse sources, such as ancient Roman villa cascades, colorful Latin American estates, modern French gardens, and Japanese Zen compositions—all crystallized in a Modernist character at Mellon Square. The adjacent U.S. Steel and Alcoa towers brought the views from above to the foreground of design considerations.

The intensive, compact design was layered with three-dimensionally nested planes unfolding to a serene interior of skydome, shimmering water, and native forest plants. As Simonds espoused, it served as a platform, structure, island, space, focal center, civic monument, gathering space, and oasis—within and separate from the city. Mellon Square was integral to reimagining Pittsburgh as a place of commerce and innovation and remains an ascendant urban space today.

By 2008, however, Mellon Square had lost the clarity of its original composition. Missing were the graceful central basin, the pastel brightness of the cascade, the continuous filigree of canopy foliage, the complete green perimeter, and the evidence of polish and care. With original design concepts discerned, the effort turned to restoring the master plan, while addressing contemporary issues.

The Pittsburgh Parks Conservancy's emphasis on balancing historic integrity, use, and maintenance provided an effective framework for preservation interventions at Mellon Square. To reinstate its richness and intricacy, the integrity of the Modernist composition had to be reestablished.

Approaching the work of a master requires insight and humility. An understanding of original design intent and execution is paramount. The Conservancy and project team chose to restore 80 percent of the plaza, while the project brief—addressing authenticity, use, function, durability, and management—led to reimagining the planter above Smithfield Street as an overlooking terrace with an adjacent green roof.

Mellon Square's transcendent character is palpable once again. It has been our challenge and pleasure to collaborate with the Conservancy, especially our valued colleagues, parks curator Susan M. Rademacher, project manager Phil Gruszka, and inspirational leader Meg Cheever, in this rebirth of Mellon Square in the great city of Pittsburgh.

Patricia M. O'Donnell, FASLA, AICP, is principal of Heritage Landscapes LLC, Preservation Landscape Architects & Planners. She led the interdisciplinary planning and design team for the Mellon Square project.

Preface

Telling the Story of a Master Work

Susan M. Rademacher

Mellon Square grabs you—with its rich layers of meaning, it rewards discovery with story upon story of a city's aspirations, an unlikely political partnership, a business district's rebirth, a groundbreaking design approach, a pioneering collaboration, a rooftop plaza, and the struggle to maintain it.

With the completion of a master plan for the plaza's restoration in 2009, what had long been suspected was at last confirmed: Mellon Square is a nationally significant designed landscape. Pittsburgh's original green roof, Mellon Square was the first Modernist garden plaza built over a parking structure, and the third park built over such a structure in the United States. Designed from the late 1940s through 1955 by architects Mitchell & Ritchey and landscape architects Simonds & Simonds, Mellon Square's aesthetic and cultural integrity is largely intact and worthy of restoration. While the two firms collaborated on the project, John O. Simonds and his brother Philip developed the specific design for the unique rooftop plaza. According to lead master planner Patricia M. O'Donnell, "its expression of urban Modernist design provides an artistic civic gathering space that adds liveliness and the beauty of human shaped nature to downtown."[1]

In 2007, after realizing that Mellon Square plays a key role in the image and value of downtown business owners and residents, the Pittsburgh Downtown Partnership invited the Pittsburgh Parks Conservancy to become involved in planning for the park's renewal. The Conservancy is a nonprofit organization founded in 1996 to improve quality of life for the people of Pittsburgh by restoring the park system to excellence with government and community partners. The organization undertakes major capital projects, restores natural areas, enlists thousands of volunteers, and provides innovative environmental education programs to children and families. Its flagship project was the $11 million conversion of a parking lot into Schenley Plaza, the grand entrance to Schenley Park. The Plaza, bordered by major cultural and educational institutions, offers a carousel, full-service restaurant, food kiosks, gardens, and great lawn to its more than five hundred thousand annual visitors. The Conservancy opened the Plaza in 2006 and operates it under a long-term lease from the City of Pittsburgh. It was the Conservancy's success with Schenley Plaza and its reputation for thoughtful park restoration projects that led the Pittsburgh Downtown Partnership to seek its assistance.

The Conservancy's first step was to bring a national expert to speak to Pittsburgh leaders. In early 2007 Charles Birnbaum, president and founder of The Cultural Landscape Foundation, inspired a rapt audience with his view of an iconic modern landscape, a masterpiece by Pittsburgh's own John O. Simonds.[2] Many of those attending expressed a keen desire to save and restore Mellon Square.

With funding from BNY Mellon, the Conservancy embarked on a planning effort in 2008. Key project partners were the Pittsburgh Parking Authority, Pittsburgh Department of Public Works, Pittsburgh Downtown Partnership, and Pittsburgh History and Landmarks Foundation. Patricia M. O'Donnell of Heritage Landscapes led the design team, which included Grenald Waldron Associates (lighting), Robert Silman Associates (structural engineering), Neil Silberman (interpretive planning, or the public presentation and discussion of a historic place's significance), and Charles Birnbaum.

The plan performed admirably by enlisting a wide array of funders for the ensuing $10 million rehabilitation and management project, which broke ground in June 2011. Heritage Landscapes led the design and construction team, which included Pfaffman + Associates (architecture), Atlantic Engineering, Hilbish McGee Lighting Design, and Mortar & ink (interpretation design).

Public outreach has also played a critical role in building awareness and appreciation of Mellon Square. The Benter Foundation has generously provided funding for a cell-phone audio tour, a concert series in the park, expanded content on the Conservancy's website, and, most significantly, producing this book on Mellon Square—the first to tell the story of this modern masterwork of landscape architecture.

The book's existence, though, owes to the inimitable impresario of cultural landscape, Charles Birnbaum, who conceived this series of monographs on seminal examples of modern landscape architecture. This particular volume would have fallen short without the valuable firsthand information and assistance provided by Simonds's colleagues Susan Simmers of EP&D, Robert Vukich and Missy Marshall of MTR Landscape Architects (an EP&D offshoot), both of whom worked on the Plaza's rehabilitation in the late 1980s. The generous personal insights of former Simonds & Simonds and Mitchell & Ritchey colleagues and associates Louis Astorino, Richard Bell, Robert Pease, Jack Scholl, and Barry Starke added depth and color to our understanding of Mellon Square's legacy. Louise Sturgess and Al Tannler of Pittsburgh History and Landmarks Foundation reviewed an early draft and helped set the record straight regarding the architect James Mitchell's lead role in the overall Mellon Square project. My superb research assistants Elaine Kramer and Julia Morrison made a huge contribution to image selection and production. Thanks also go to Meredith Baber, who gave exacting attention to every word as my editor at Princeton Architectural Press.

My deepest appreciation goes to the spirited Marjorie Simonds, who so graciously offered her personal memories, family albums, and John's original journals as further research for this book. In the course of sixty-three years of marriage to John, she shared his passionate mission to better the earth. Before her death in 2012, Marjorie generously shared her personal perspectives and family mementoes, channeling her husband's mantras as clearly as a bell in a Zen temple garden.

Prologue

The Simonds Way

Richard C. Bell, FASLA, FAAR

I will always think of John Simonds as a Zen Buddhist master; like the Buddhists, he was always searching for harmony in his work. I was very fortunate to become his apprentice in 1950, as there were very few apprenticeships available in our profession.

When John hired me, he realized that I was in line to win the Rome Prize fellowship in Landscape Architecture in 1951. In 1950 I had turned down the fellowship, stating to my jurors that I had a position at Simonds & Simonds in Pittsburgh and felt if I had fifteen months of apprenticeship, I would be better able to profit from the American Academy in Rome. They agreed, as they had great respect for the Simonds firm. In 1948 the firm had hired George Patton, who won the Rome Prize after serving in their office, so they had a certain pride in my desiring to win it.

There were two masters in this office—John and Philip. John was the "outside man," pursuing work, and the primary designer, and Philip was the "inside man," hammering out working drawings and supervising construction.

The Simonds way of drafting was to use pen and ink on tracing linen. All lettering would be in ink with the use of a Leroy drafting machine (a simple, consistent lettering tool) for most of our technical jargon. Our India ink was broken down into five gradations and our strongest and blackest lines would represent the most important information of the drawing. There was no question which office turned out the most professional drawings in Pittsburgh—ours.

John taught a night course in site planning to the architectural students at Carnegie Tech. He wanted to teach the important relationship between landscape architecture and architecture, hopeful that as architects they would use this knowledge in their future work. His second semester course included factual knowledge and site planning principles, of interest to most urban and regional planners. He reappraised the city and region in terms of planning a more efficient, productive, and pleasant environment for people.

Philip Simonds was a master in his own right. He was a graduate civil engineer who in World War II was assigned to the Pacific Theater as a Seabee. He knew the core nuts and bolts of site planning and engineering, and I learned from him. Working drawings became second nature to me. I attribute my abilities as a landscape architect to the fact that I seriously learned the Simonds Way. Pen-and-ink drawing became my staff of life.

John believed in harmony, and our office was run in this manner. I never heard an ill word spoken by any of us in the office.

John was a natural leader and world traveler who respected God, nature, and people. Truly knowledgeable about our profession, he diligently pursued it through his work ethic. He was learning all the time and taught this trait to me. His second lesson was to learn the difference between a numbers system and a value system—it is far more important to sell the client on their project's intrinsic value than to bombard them with numbers and cost-benefit ratios.

He was a true environmentalist long before others began to grasp this concept. Time and again he impressed upon me that as landscape architects we must be the masters of environmental design. This would be our true value on design teams of artists, architects, and engineers, culminating in superior design solutions.

I heard you well, John! We are all chips off of your block.[1]

Richard C. Bell, an advocate for the arts and landscape architecture, founded the Bell/Glazener Design Group, a landscape architecture firm based in Raleigh, North Carolina.

1

Designing
Experiences

When it opened in 1955, Mellon Square represented Pittsburgh's quest to reinvent itself as a modern city by managing the glut of automobiles and providing verdant public space. It took an extraordinary design team, the architects Mitchell & Ritchey and the landscape architects Simonds & Simonds, to meet both needs in one unified composition of underground parking garage and rooftop plaza. [FIG. 1] Both Mitchell & Ritchey and Simonds & Simonds had positioned themselves within the Allegheny Conference on Community Development (ACCD), fostered through their many commissions to design the private homes and landscapes of wealthy and influential leaders within the community. Mitchell & Ritchey's 1947 report for Kaufmann's Department Store, *Pittsburgh in Progress*, signaled their imaginative command of the modern urban city and attracted the interest of prominent city leaders, politicians, and businessmen.[1] This design team was the Pittsburgh region's most significant long-term design collaboration of the modern era.

FIG. 2
James A. Mitchell and Dahlen K.
Ritchey display their model and
plan for redeveloping the Lower Hill
District with the Civic Arena as its
centerpiece.

Mitchell & Ritchey

Realizing the pioneering garage structure was Mitchell & Ritchey, a
dominant firm in Pittsburgh and a principal advocate for modern architecture in the 1940s and 1950s. [FIG. 2] James A. Mitchell (1907–1999)
and Dahlen K. Ritchey (1910–2002) became friends as architecture students at Carnegie Mellon University, graduating in 1932 with Ritchey first
in the class. Mitchell received a master of architecture from Columbia
University in 1933. That year, Mitchell received a gold medal from the
Beaux-Arts Institute of Design and was a finalist for the Paris Prize in
Architecture. Also a finalist for the Paris Prize in 1933, Ritchey pursued
his graduate degree at Harvard University's Graduate School of Design
(GSD) where he was influenced by Professor Walter Gropius, the influential Modernist architect and founder of the Bauhaus in Germany.
The GSD was founded by Dean Joseph Hudnut, who was regarded as
"a guiding light in the quest to invent an American Modernism in the
fields of architecture and city design."[2] Hudnut had brought Gropius
to Harvard in the early days of the "Harvard Revolution" against the

authoritative Beaux-Arts traditions. Their ideas of modern architecture and urbanism diverged and Hudnut's leadership of the movement was soon eclipsed. [FIG. 3]

FIG. 3
Walter Gropius, shown in 1954, led the Modernist revolution at Harvard's Graduate School of Design.

This movement transfigured the design professions by taking inspiration from natural forms and modern art, and promoting asymmetry and informality. After graduation, both Mitchell and Ritchey received travelling fellowships to study European architecture. Their meetings with prominent modern architects would prove to be a strong influence on their later works in Pittsburgh.[3] Upon return to Pittsburgh, Ritchey landed a job designing window and furnishing displays for Kaufmann's Department Store, the beginning of a providential association with Edgar Kaufmann Sr.

The two young architects made a splash in the 1937 journal of the Pittsburgh Architectural Club with a two-part article that posed the question, "Does architecture as practiced today express the spirit of our time?"[4] In 1938 Mitchell & Ritchey went into practice together, with their first office located just around the corner from the future site of Mellon Square. Their practice was interrupted by wartime service from 1943 to 1946. Both served in the Navy, where Mitchell's exceptional talent for industrial-scale planning emerged in his post of chief of the facilities and services section of the Naval Ordnance Establishments Division.

Resuming their architectural practice after the war, Mitchell & Ritchey established the firm as "the principal advocate for modern architecture in Pittsburgh during the 1940s and 1950s.... [Mitchell] was the lead design architect in the firm and deserves primary credit for the firm's assertive and sometimes innovative modern design work."[5] Their portfolio included schools, housing projects, corporate office buildings, health care facilities, campus buildings, and a number of large-scale redevelopment projects during the Pittsburgh Renaissance. One of their most significant works—and their final project as partners—was the Civic Arena, now demolished, in collaboration with Simonds & Simonds

FIG. 4
Mitchell & Ritchey and Simonds & Simonds collaborated on this concept for redeveloping the Lower Hill District, setting its arena centerpiece within a rich frame of green space.

FIG. 5
Mitchell & Ritchey appraise a sample section of one-and-a-half stories of stamped aluminum panel proposed for Alcoa's skyscraper, 1951.

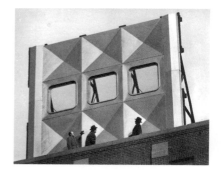

and completed in 1962 as part of the visionary scheme to redevelop the Lower Hill District. [FIG. 4] Mitchell had received a patent for an early version of the Arena's domed aluminum roof—the largest clear span of its time, retracting to a single point. Frequently associated with internationally prominent architects, the firm teamed with design architect Harrison & Abramovitz for both the Alcoa Building and the U.S. Steel/ Mellon Bank Building, significant modern buildings designed and constructed in tandem with Mellon Square. [FIG. 5]

When the Mitchell & Ritchey partnership dissolved in 1957, it was agreed that Mitchell would receive 100 percent of the credit for design, and would share 50 percent of the credit for production and administration with Ritchey.[6] After Mitchell relocated to Connecticut in 1957, Ritchey continued with his practice as D. K. Ritchey Associates and, in 1959, formed Deeter & Ritchey with Russell O. Deeter. The firm became Deeter Ritchey Sippel Associates in 1965 when longtime associate William "Fritz" Sippel was named partner. Significant clients included Westinghouse, Carnegie Mellon University, and the University of Pittsburgh. Ritchey's ongoing collaborations with Simonds & Simonds included the Renaissance redevelopment projects for the seventy-eight-acre Allegheny Center and Three Rivers Stadium, now demolished. Today, the firm continues to practice as DRS Architects.

Simonds & Simonds

Leading the design of Mellon Square's rooftop plaza, Simonds & Simonds was among the twentieth century's most influential landscape architectural and environmental planning firms. Cofounders John O. Simonds (1913–2005) and Philip D. Simonds (1916–1995) renamed the firm as Environmental Planning and Design (EP&D) in 1969 to reflect its expansion into groundbreaking environmental planning for new communities. [FIG. 6] Among his many writings, John O. Simonds authored the authoritative textbook *Landscape Architecture*, first published in 1961, that remains a required reference for the profession to this day.[7]

Recognized as one of the most influential landscape architects of the second half of the twentieth century, Simonds was a pioneer of the Modernist movement within the profession—both as an author and a designer. Simonds was born in Jamestown, North Dakota, in 1913 and later moved with his family to Michigan. A sickly child, Simonds was so skinny that he was nicknamed "Slats." He attended a "fresh-air school" for a regime of outdoor exercise, good food, and naps. His father was a Methodist preacher and his mother was artistic, encouraging John and his two brothers and sister to enjoy nature and live robustly. [FIG. 7]

Simonds studied landscape architecture at the University of Michigan, taking a year off to live in Borneo and travel throughout Asia. [FIG. 8] After he graduated in 1935 with a bachelor's degree in landscape architecture, he went on to study for a master's degree in landscape architecture at the GSD, where he won a gold medal for drawing.[8] [FIGS. 9 AND 10] A 1999 letter from Simonds recalled his time at Harvard:

> Whenever I try to sing the Yale Whiffenpoof song, which isn't all that often, I never get as far as the "tables down at Mory's"...I always get hung up on that bit about where the

FIG. 6
Philip and John O. Simonds
established one of the nation's
foremost landscape architecture
firms.

FIG. 7
John O. Simonds, shown at age
seven in Michigan, was called
"Ormsbee" as a child.

FIG. 8
Simonds's sketches from his
Asian travels included this scene
in Borneo.

FIG. 9
Simonds applied his meticulous
hand in studio at the Harvard
Graduate School of Design.

FIG. 10
Simonds had a reputation for
cartooning on the chalkboard
during charrettes at Harvard. Note
Simon still sketches city sites at
center of image—his surname was
spelled "Simon" until the brothers
established their practice in
Pittsburgh.

"little black sheep have gone astray"...and my mind goes
back to Robinson Hall and Harvard in the '30s.

Those were the deep depression years. If ever
there was a flock of "poor little lambs who had lost their
way," it was we....As students of landscape architecture,
we had strayed off the glistening Beaux-Arts avenue and im-
perious Renaissance axis. We were lost in the thorny under-
brush somewhere between Haffner Woods, Walden Pond,
and the Bauhaus.

We lost not only our potential clients, the Vanderbilt
types with their great estates and posh resorts, we lost our
very profession. When I asked my mentor, Dr. Gropius, what
role he saw for landscape architecture in contemporary society, he looked at me long and thoughtfully without speaking.
It was quite possibly one of the most eloquent statement[s]
ever never stated.

We LA students were searching then, all of us,
for a more compelling direction in our field. We had a fever-
ish sense of mission with no definable cause. When told by
a visiting lecturer that our work was beautification and our
watchword beauty, we walked out of the room. Faced with
decrepit and sagging cities, urban sprawl, and the trashing
of the landscape, we had better things to do with our lives,
but we didn't quite know what....In the decades that had
followed the tumultuous GSD "revolution" the practice of
landscape architecture has progressed by quantum leaps.[9]

Modernist principles instilled at Harvard became a founda-
tional aspect of the work of both Simonds & Simonds and Mitchell &
Ritchey. Simonds absorbed the Harvard Revolution's principles for landscape architecture, in which space was to be structured by plantings,
low maintenance was a pragmatic goal, and modern building materials
like concrete and stainless steel were introduced to the palette. Simonds
counted both Gropius and Dean Joseph Hudnut as mentors. It is evident
from Simonds's practice and writings that he was shaped by Hudnut's
principles and interests.

FIG. 11
Dean Joseph Hudnut, founder of the Graduate School of Design at Harvard University, had a profound influence on Simonds's values and career direction.

FIG. 12
Marjorie and John O. Simonds, ca. 1943.

[Hudnut took] a humanistic approach to design that expressed "emotional content," as he liked to say—spontaneity, symbolic values, individual concerns.... Creating an urban pattern that worked to foster social harmony and to satisfy individual needs and the needs of the human spirit in a world increasingly shaped by industrialization, cars, and suburbanization—this was the focus of Hudnut's efforts at Harvard, and it was the reason he had founded the GSD.[10]

After receiving his master's in landscape architecture in 1939, Simonds traveled with fellow Harvard graduate Lester A. Collins (1914–1993) on an extended trip throughout Asia.[11] Simonds would later recount a deep appreciation for Asian design and philosophy through his explorations. Out of this period came his lifelong conviction that "One designs not places, or spaces or things—one designs experiences."[12]

Following his travels abroad, Simonds considered locating his practice in Seattle. Hudnut advised him, "In the Pacific Northwest, God will be your competition; in Pittsburgh you are needed."[14] [FIG. 11] As Simonds's wife Marjorie later recalled, "Dean Hudnut also noted that 'Garden clubs will be allies, so you must go and speak to them, bring them along, take your message to the masses about what landscape architecture is.'"[15] Simonds's brothers Dick, an executive with Pittsburgh Plate Glass (PPG), and Philip were already in Pittsburgh. Phil had graduated from the University of Michigan with a degree in civil engineering and established a solo private practice in Pittsburgh. When John moved to Pittsburgh he immediately teamed with Phil to establish Simonds & Simonds. Soon after, he met Marjorie Todd and they were married in 1943.[16] [FIG. 12]

Initially, Simonds & Simonds focused on residential projects, playgrounds, public schools, and parks. John tended to look at the big picture, while Phil had a gift for details. The brothers' early commissions were to design domestic landscapes and gardens for Pittsburghers. As a result, the beginnings of the firm were humble and finances limited. Their first office was also their walk-up apartment above a Chinese restaurant. As commissions came in, they moved to a second-story space at 219 Montgomery Street in the North Side neighborhood of Pittsburgh. On the first floor was the architectural firm Button and McLean, which gave the young landscape architects work in site planning for government sponsored wartime housing for the influx of steel workers during World War II. Employees in both offices enjoyed their proximity to Allegheny Commons, built in 1867, across the street. Thus the city's first public greenspace gave the young Simonds brothers an early taste of the benefits of having a public park as a source of workday refreshment.

It was a stunning accomplishment for the Simonds brothers to move from walk-up offices above an architecture firm to their ultimate headquarters at 100 Ross Street, which was locally admired for its interior greenery, sculpture, and innovative workspaces. The firm's involvement in Pittsburgh's "Renaissance I" earned the firm national recognition. Among their notable local projects were the Equitable Life Insurance Plaza (1955), Greater Pittsburgh Airport (1952), the Pittsburgh Aviary-Conservatory (1967), and the Civic Arena (1961). The Equitable Plaza, also built over a parking garage like its contemporary Mellon Square, was designed in collaboration with the New York City–based firm Clarke & Rapuano as part of the Gateway Center Development at Pittsburgh's Golden Triangle. With modern office buildings set within a lush landscape, Equitable Plaza is considered Pittsburgh's premiere example of International Style planning. [FIG. 13]

The Pittsburgh Aviary-Conservatory, built by the City of Pittsburgh in 1952, was celebrated for its 1967 expansion, which featured innovative displays of wildlife and plants depicting native settings including the "wetlands room," designed by Simonds & Simonds.[17] [FIG. 14] The Aviary is located within Pittsburgh's oldest park, Allegheny Commons, for which Simonds & Simonds completed a long-range development plan in 1966. Their plan reimagined the picturesque Lake Elizabeth as a trapezoidal concrete-lined pool with embedded stream boulders and crossed by a pair of arched pedestrian bridges that meet on a small island. The Simonds & Simonds plan has been described as "a high modern reaffirmation of West Common as a pastoral landscape," instead of "retreating from more drastic interventions and preserving the park's underlying, original emphasis on pastoral design and passive recreation, Pittsburgh's urban renewal planners showed unusual sensitivity to the one hundred-year-old landscape they were charged with renewing."[18] [FIG. 15]

Also in the 1960s, Simonds & Simonds was one of three Pittsburgh firms to design a system of new regional parks for Allegheny County.[20] In the vein of designing and planning for public open spaces, Simonds and his partners developed the first master plan for the Chicago Botanic Garden in 1961. Subsequent work for the garden extended through construction and its opening in 1972, as well as multiple additional projects. Their innovative use of the site's natural wetlands to create a series of linked lagoons as an educational garden influenced the design of botanic gardens around the country. For Simonds functionality was inherently tied to aesthetics:

> Beauty. It's a misunderstood word. It's a word that landscape architects and architects and physical planners, they have to build back into their vocabulary. Beautiful. Can't be ashamed to say it, if I think it's beautiful or a place is beautiful, it's beautiful. Beauty by definition is a perceived harmonious relationship of all the elements....If something is working well together, if all the parts are functioning well and you can't think of any way to improve that space or that place or that form, to perform that function, it is per se beautiful. The ugly is the presence of one or more incompatible or non-working parts.[21]

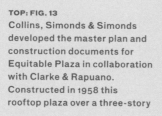

underground parking garage was modeled after Simonds's work at Mellon Square; the building architect was Max Abramovitz for Harrison & Abramovitz.

TOP: FIG. 13
Collins, Simonds & Simonds developed the master plan and construction documents for Equitable Plaza in collaboration with Clarke & Rapuano. Constructed in 1958 this rooftop plaza over a three-story

BOTTOM LEFT: FIG. 14
Simonds & Simonds designed the innovative immersion interior at Pittsburgh Aviary-Conservatory in 1953, and the expansion in 1967.

BOTTOM RIGHT: FIG. 15
Simonds gave Lake Elizabeth in historic Allegheny Commons a modern reinvention.

As Simonds said, "Our approach to all project planning and design—no matter the type or scale—is PCD (Preserve, Conserve, and only then Develop)."[22] This philosophy included preserving an area's natural resources, such as wetlands, and confining development to less sensitive areas, and is exemplified in the firm's award-winning Comprehensive Master Plan for Pelican Bay, the 2,100-acre planned community in Florida, dating to the 1970s. Though common in practice today, this approach was revolutionary in its time.

John O. Simonds was highly regarded by his peers and received substantial recognition. For his contributions to the profession, he was inducted as a Fellow of the ASLA in 1965. He was awarded the ASLA Medal in 1973, and in 1999 received a most fitting tribute—the ASLA President's Centennial Medal on the one-hundredth anniversary of the founding of ASLA. Simonds died in Pittsburgh in May 2005 at age ninety-two. He is internationally regarded as one of the truly great twentieth-century landscape architects—in practice, education, and service. As he asked in a 1998 commentary:

> What then is this sense of mission that has guided us for the past one hundred years and into the next generation? It is the belief that the work of the landscape architect is to help bring the things people do, the structures they build, and the way they live into a more compatible and rewarding relationship with the living landscape of planet Earth.[24]

2

The Genesis of Mellon Square: Design for a New Era

Downtown Pittsburgh today is favored with a fine assortment of outdoor spaces. But in 1945, to returning veterans or up-and-coming executives mulling over a move to "Smoketown," it was bereft of green, asphyxiating, and clogged with cars.

Just a decade later, a serene oasis would appear—not as a mirage, but as the harbinger of a remade city and a precursor of the green roof movement. Pittsburghers warmly embraced their new Mellon Square, with the convenience of a parking garage tucked below and retail shopping at street level. Its refreshing design was meant to convey, in an elegantly modern style, the sense of a mountain glade centered on a spring-fed pool, with a stream tumbling down to the city. [FIG. 16] The asymmetrical placement of planters and basins offered visitors a well-ordered and varied experience, from bustling corridors to mingling spaces to quiet alcoves. Catching all these elements in its weave was an intricate pavement patterned in overlapping triangles shaded white, grey, green, and black. This composition energized the plaza's ground plane and made for a fascinating scene when viewed from the windows of surrounding buildings.[1]

Sixty years later Mellon Square stands as a pioneering example of a park designed and constructed in conjunction with a subterranean parking facility. It is the first to have been conceived and constructed as a single unified design. Pittsburgh had been working toward this solution through a decade of parking studies, starting in 1939. The Pittsburgh Regional Planning Association (RPA) published a 1946 report noting, "the automobile had become the dominant form of transportation in the central business district by 1937. The precipitous decline of property values and closing down of many small businesses was related to the lack of parking space."[2] The RPA recommended the future site of Mellon Square as one of five sites for the initial public-parking program

FIG. 16
The parking facility, retail space,
and rooftop plaza were conceived
as a single design.

that culminated in the 1949 plan for a "parking park" on the site that
would be developed as Mellon Square.[3] This report presented a synthe-
sis of downtown infrastructure needs in its vision for a "stepped level"
garage, widened adjacent streets, new stores and restaurants, and a
sloping, terraced park.

America's first known parking structure was built in 1918 for the
Hotel LaSalle in Chicago, but it took only twenty years for the dramatic
rise in automobile ownership to press cities toward underground solutions.[4] Cities viewed their downtown parkland as the opportune locations
for such developments. Until Mellon Square, all the early underground
structures had been built under historic squares. Union Square in San
Francisco is generally considered the world's first underground structure, designed by Timothy Pfleuger and built in 1942 under a park dating

from 1850.[5] Also in San Francisco, a subterranean garage and new park opened in 1960 on the site of the historic Portsmouth Square.[6] In Los Angeles, the nineteenth-century Pershing Square was demolished in 1952 to build an underground eighteen-hundred-car parking garage with a park on top. Upon the project's completion, the new Pershing Square featured a lawn panel to which reflecting pools were later added.[7]

These hybrid parking parks were an innovative means of creating new downtown public spaces for postwar America. For decades, they have given welcome relief to the dense urban fabric and have accrued cultural and economic value. As a testament to its significance, Mellon Square was listed as a contributing property to the Pittsburgh Central Downtown Historic District in the National Register of Historic Places in 2013.[8] The American Planning Association named it one of "America's Ten Great Public Spaces" in 2008. According to American Planning Association Executive Director Paul Farmer, a former deputy planning director in Pittsburgh, "The Square is iconic not only for its design and character, but for the way it was planned and the role it played in spurring revitalization and private investment in Downtown Pittsburgh."[9]

A Strategic Spot in the Downtown Fabric

Peeling back the layers of time adds depth to the experience of a place—from how the land itself was formed, to the makers of the city grid that formed Mellon Square, to the postwar effort that made Pittsburgh into an appealing city again for citizens and tourists. [FIG. 17] A brief biographical sketch of Mellon Square's single city block provides a useful context for appreciating the modern masterwork.

From the design point of view, there are both practical and poetic reasons to understand a place by exploring its past. A design that can stand the test of time must be an intelligent response to the many conditions a site presents. Among these are landform, drainage, microclimate, neighboring streets and buildings, and social use. A structure as massive and deep as Mellon Square's six-story parking garage had to be carefully embedded into its site in the floodplain where two rivers unite.

Many people think of Pittsburgh as a mountainous landscape, but Pittsburgh's hills are actually the residue of an ancient plateau,

FIG. 17
Mellon Square presented a
welcome open space in the midst
of Pittsburgh's urban high-rise
landscape, ca. 1955.

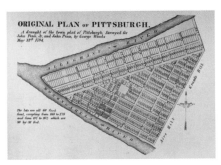

FIG. 18
This is the first known illustration
of Pittsburgh, by George Beck,
painted ca. 1804.

FIG. 19
Oriented to both riverfronts, the
city's grid was platted in 1784.

carved and recarved by rivers and streams in the slowness of geographic time. (One of these prehistoric streambeds lies beneath Mellon Square.) The wedge of land known as "the Point" was formed by the deposition of alluvial soils where the Allegheny and Monongahela rivers met. This dynamic and rich landscape was home to a succession of native peoples, beginning with the hunter-gatherers as early as sixteen thousand years ago. The region's last dominant native culture was the Late Woodland period (1000–1500 CE), whose traders and warriors gave name to the places and trails that were adopted by Colonial settlers from the early 1700s on.[10]

At the confluence of the Allegheny and Monongahela Rivers, the Point was eagerly encroached upon by the French and the British who built their forts to exploit the military advantages of the forks of the Ohio River. Accompanying improvements around the forts soon established the pioneer town of Pittsburgh, and in the space of a few decades its occupants came to dominate the American industrial age owing to a blockbuster combination of strategic location, abundant natural resources, and human ingenuity. [FIG. 18]

Mellon Square occupies one block in the city grid, which was laid out in the 1784 survey by George Woods and assistant Thomas Vickroy on a commission by the Penn family.[11] Because Pittsburgh wanted to make the most of its frontage on two rivers, the street grid was oriented to both waterfronts. The grids were joined along Liberty Street where triangular lots resolved the two geometries. [FIG. 19]

A single "Market Square" (also known as "the Diamond") was carved out of the grid and was the only public open space in the business district for nearly 150 years. The city's first courthouse was built there in 1794, facing a semicircular structure for vendor stalls. When a new courthouse was completed a few blocks away in 1841, the square returned to its sole purpose as a market until a devastating downtown fire destroyed it in 1845. A pair of mid-nineteenth-century brick market buildings from 1852 were replaced in 1914 by the New Diamond Market occupying all four quadrants of the square, but with openings to allow Diamond Street to pass diagonally through the square.[12] To the east stood Grant's Hill, which rose abruptly from the grid and soon became the city's pleasure ground and site for civic celebrations. But by the early twentieth century, the hill's lower slope had become a detrimental "hump" interrupting street traffic and thwarting further development, and so it was removed.[13]

By that time, people had long been referring to the triangular floodplain between the Allegheny and Monongahela Rivers as the "Golden Triangle." Mayor William J. Howard reportedly first used the phrase after the fire of 1845, when he said, "We shall make of this triangle of blackened ruins a golden triangle whose fame will endure as a priceless heritage."[14] Over the next century, Pittsburgh's urban form was shaped and reshaped by its economic, social, and political evolution.

Pittsburgh's Downtown Decline and Renaissance

By 1900 the city's riverfront landscape had been transformed into a vast industrial expanse to support the production of glass, iron, steel, and oil. Though the great industrialists Andrew Carnegie, Henry Clay Frick, and Henry J. Heinz had developed their manufacturing complexes along river edges, company headquarters were located in downtown Pittsburgh within the grid of the central business district. Less than a mile from the Point, near Fifth Avenue and Smithfield Street, stood the hub of the Mellon banking empire at the heart of the city's financial and commercial center. In 1869 Judge Thomas Mellon housed his new bank in the block adjacent to the future site of Mellon Square. The block was bounded by Smithfield Street, Sixth Avenue, and two alleys, which later became William Penn Place and Oliver Avenue. Over the years the

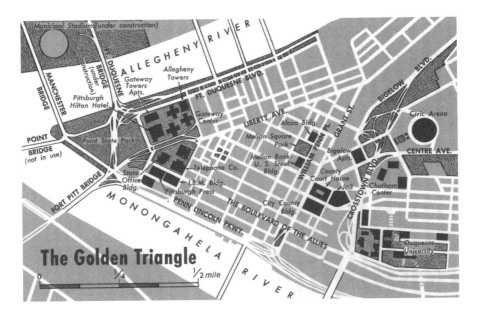

FIG. 20
Pittsburgh's central business district has been known as the "Golden Triangle" since 1845.

block contained a mix of large and small multistory buildings housing businesses, including Peoples Natural Gas Building, the Davis Theatre, and the Dispatch. Over time, Mellon Bank moved into new buildings, but always within the same block. Several Mellon-owned businesses got their start in these buildings, such as Gulf Oil Corporation, Koppers Company, and the Aluminum Company of America (Alcoa).

From the late nineteenth century into the early twentieth century, the city's leaders routinely commissioned renowned planners and architects to build a civic legacy, including H. H. Richardson, Frank Furness, George Post, Frederick Law Olmsted Jr., Frank Lloyd Wright, and Robert Moses. Pittsburgh's greatest concentration of these prominent commercial and institutional buildings is found in the central downtown area, including works by Daniel H. Burnham (Oliver Building), Henry Hornbostel (Smithfield United Church), Benno Janssen (William Penn Hotel), F. J. Osterling (Union Arcade Building), George B. Post (Park Building), and Trowbridge and Livingston (Mellon Bank).[15] The 1.3-acre Mellon Square would come to be nested within the epicenter of this remarkable collection of architectural works. [FIG. 20]

FIG. 21
The "Smoky City" was densely
blanketed with smog prior to
Pennsylvania's enactment of
the nation's first smoke control
legislation.

Rapidly coating Pittsburgh's handsome buildings was a layer of black soot, starkly contrasting the city's cultural aspirations with the gritty basis of its strength. Thick, dark smog and soot hanging in the air over the surrounding river valleys was the byproduct of Pittsburgh's success. In the years between the World Wars, the air was so smoky that drivers sometimes turned on their headlights in midmorning. American Sign Language even had a gesture— flicking imaginary soot from the shoulder—that signified Pittsburgh.[16] Although the Steel City's dirty image was a symbol of wealth to industrialists and of job security to the working class, it was a barrier to attracting new residents. [FIG. 21]

The stock market crash of 1929 and the ensuing Great Depression hit Pittsburgh industries hard. Five years later, one-third of the city's population was still unemployed, despite New Deal employment opportunities. Even with Pittsburgh's industrial capacity to produce glass, iron, steel, and oil called upon to support the American effort in World War II, the city's recovery was precarious.

Throughout this period, Pittsburgh's national profile was dimming. In 1930 *Harper's Magazine* asked "Is Pittsburgh Civilized?"[17] In 1944 Pittsburgh was rated a "class D" city by the *Wall Street Journal*.[18] Property values in the Golden Triangle were dropping by a staggering $10 million each year, with a 40 percent vacancy rate for office space.[19] Both the perception and the reality of poor environmental conditions, annual floods, and substandard housing were crippling the vigorous city.

Mellon Confronts the Problem

Richard King Mellon, grandson of Thomas Mellon and chairman of what had become one of America's largest banks, was directly confronted with this issue when, in 1941, he returned to active military duty in the U.S. Army (having previously served in World War I and remained in the Reserves) and initiated a national search for executives to head the businesses of his conglomerate empire. However, "he found that most of the highly capable men he sought had no interest in moving to 'smoky Pittsburgh.' And if they did, their wives balked."[20] [FIG. 22] Mellon realized that if a new image could not be created to retain current businesses and attract future employees and executives, even the corporations of the Mellon empire would be forced to relocate.

FIG. 22
Constance and Richard King Mellon.

Mellon has been called a reluctant leader. A shy college dropout, he went to work for the family business as a messenger. He assumed control of the family's banking empire after the 1933 death of his father, Richard Beatty Mellon. Most of Western Pennsylvania's large companies were launched with Mellon backing, including Alcoa, Gulf Oil, Heinz, Koppers, U.S. Steel, and Westinghouse Air Brake. While the necessity of protecting the family's business interests certainly drove Mellon into civic leadership, he was, no doubt, inspired by his late father's pride in Pittsburgh.

Pittsburgh desperately needed the highest level of leadership to bring about the city's new image. Its clean air and civic revitalization project became known as the "Pittsburgh Renaissance." This transformative era, from 1946 to 1970, is now referred to as "Renaissance I." It was followed by a second campaign of reinvention, informally dubbed "Renaissance II," that began with the 1976 election of Mayor Richard S. Caliguiri in response to the collapse of the steel industry and the oil crisis. Some Pittsburghers have even begun to refer to the third wave of building projects that began in 1994 with the Tom Murphy mayoral administration as "Renaissance III."

The city's first Renaissance required a leadership approach that cut across traditional boundaries, in which leaders of commerce and industry partnered with design professionals and government officials to envision Pittsburgh's Golden Triangle as a vibrant urban core. They aimed to combat the pervasive picture of the dirty "Steel City," promoting a new and progressive image by putting a bold scheme for urban renewal into action.

FIG. 23
Pittsburgh's Point was rife
with derelict structures before
demolition, ca. 1935–36.

Yet by 1946 despite these new forces
and a growing number of plans to redesign the
central business district, Westinghouse, Alcoa,
and U.S. Steel had made plans to relocate their
offices to other cities. In a bold preemptive move, Mellon and his cousin
Paul Mellon solicited architects Mitchell & Ritchey and landscape architects Simonds & Simonds to conceive of a grand complex that would
house Alcoa and the expanded Mellon Bank operations in twin towers,
facing each other across a park. The design team was asked to incor-
porate underground parking for the Pittsburgh Parking Authority (PPA)
based on previous traffic studies that had slated the block for this use.

The physical results were transformational. Major buildings
constructed that were contiguous with the future Mellon Square site
included the forty-one-story U.S. Steel/Mellon Bank Tower in 1950 and
the thirty-story Alcoa Building in 1951. Within four years Mellon Square
would be complete. With its garden plaza, largely designed by Simonds
& Simonds, built atop a six-story subterranean garage designed
by Mitchell & Ritchey, the Square was the catalyst for a celebratory
urban image of the city. At the same time, a wholesale conversion was

FIG. 24
After Pittsburgh's Renaissance,
Point State Park reclaimed the city's
most valuable and historic territory
for public enjoyment, ca. 1969.

underway to convert the derelict Point into a thirty-seven-acre state park.[21]

Less than a year after plans were announced for Mellon Square, the physical renewal of the city began on May 18, 1950, with the first buildings demolished for Point State Park, on the former site of Fort Pitt. [FIGS. 23 AND 24] From 1950 to the mid-1960s, more than 25 percent of the 330 acres of the Golden Triangle, including the block of Mellon Square, were rebuilt and improved as a result of the Renaissance envisioned by the ACCD. At the end of the period, half a billion dollars were spent in one of the most intensive peacetime reconstruction initiatives of any city center in the country.

All the Renaissance projects depended on several key drivers. These included the patronage of department store mogul Edgar Kaufmann, the leadership of Mellon and Mayor David L. Lawrence, as well as the formation of the ACCD and of the PPA.

FIG. 25
Margaret Bourke-White's photo-
graph of Mayor Lawrence and R. K.
Mellon appeared in *Life* magazine,
May 1956.

Mayor Lawrence Leads

David Leo Lawrence (1889–1966) grew up in
the Golden Triangle as a working-class child.
His political career commenced after service in
World War I, when he was elected chairman of the struggling Allegheny
County Democratic Party. After Franklin Delano Roosevelt's victory in
the 1931 presidential election, Lawrence took the lead in gaining control
of federal patronage for Pittsburgh and helped to elect the state's first
Democratic governor in the twentieth century. Political appointments
followed for Lawrence, including secretary of the Commonwealth and
state chairman of the Democratic Party.

In 1945 Lawrence was elected the city's first democratic
mayor since the turn of the century. After the election Mellon, a reso-
lute republican, called upon the new mayor to offer congratulations.
This unlikely pair found common ground on behalf of their city, forging
a highly effective partnership to advance the Renaissance. [FIG. 25]

Upon taking office, the mayor's seven-point program to
improve Pittsburgh was one of the nation's first urban renewal plans.

Lawrence's 1946 decision to enforce the Smoke Control Ordinance (1941) burdened the working class population because it raised their cost of living and endangered jobs. Despite protests, however, Lawrence was resoundingly reelected in 1949. Playing a vital role in engaging local political powers with civic leaders, he served four terms as mayor until 1959 when he was elected Pennsylvania's thirty-seventh governor. In his view of Pittsburgh's Renaissance, Mayor Lawrence wrote, "Our grand design in Pittsburgh has been the acceptance of a belief that a city is worth saving…"[22]

Allegheny Conference on Community Development
Virtually no new public or private amenities had been built within Pittsburgh from 1929 to 1945, creating a daunting backlog of long-overdue improvement needs for infrastructure and building stock. Combined with the increase of the automobile as the dominant form of transportation, a lack of parking spaces was a major issue for the health and vitality of the many small businesses in the downtown area.

In response, an economic development organization agency was formed in 1943 with financial backing by Mellon.[23] The ACCD was a powerful force in Pittsburgh's rebirth. It had three clear goals: improve air quality through industrial smoke control, control downtown flooding, and revitalize downtown through a series of urban improvements.

These goals—in both reality and image—were essential to positioning the city as healthy, vibrant, and cultured. Starting with smoke control legislation, the measures taken in due course helped to keep and attract corporate businesses. As ACCD executive director Park H. Martin noted, "If 'Downtown' is to continue to hold its own with suburban shopping centers, it must have sufficient well located parking lots or garages."[24]

The success of the ACCD was in part due to close ties to leading planning and research agencies and a complex network of prominent individuals in various government positions, agencies, and authorities. The predominantly republican ACCD was able to strategically align with democratic city and state politicians thanks to the leadership of Mayor Lawrence, who achieved the bipartisan consensus necessary to secure funding and advance the ambitious projects.

The ACCD continued to sponsor detailed plans by local landscape architects, architects, and engineers throughout the late 1950s and 1960s. Among them, Mitchell & Ritchey and Simonds & Simonds were commissioned to produce design ideas, sketches, and plans for downtown renewal projects, including Equitable Plaza at the Gateway Center and the Civic Arena with its innovative retractable aluminum roof. The concepts generated by these design professionals increased the effectiveness of the ACCD, and enhanced the designers' stature. As a result, the ACCD evolved from an advocate for policy planning to an action-oriented organization equipped with plans and sketches showing what Pittsburgh could become. As projects to improve economic vitality within the city were completed from the 1950s through the 1960s, the ACCD chronicled its success with the publication *Pittsburgh and Allegheny County: An Era of Progress and Accomplishment.*

A powerful partner in these efforts was created when the Urban Redevelopment Authority of Pittsburgh (URA)—the nation's first such governmental agency—was founded in November 1946 to carry out major municipal development projects and programs. Under the leadership of executive director John P. Robin, the URA worked effectively with the ACCD to transform the city through high-impact projects such as Point State Park, Gateway Center, the modernization of Jones & Laughlin Steel Corporation's South Side works, Children's Hospital, the Civic Arena, East Liberty, and Allegheny Center on Pittsburgh's North Side.

Parking Comes Into Focus

Civic leaders also confronted head-on the need for more public parking along with an authority to manage it. In 1947 the ACCD helped prepare the "Pittsburgh Package" of ten legislative bills, which included enabling legislation to establish the PPA.

Also working on this issue was the RPA, which produced a report in 1946 relating the lack of downtown parking to the "precipitous decline of property values and closing down of many small businesses."[25] The report recommended the future Mellon Square as one of five sites suggested for the initial public parking program. In April 1949 the organization presented the city with "Parking Park Study: A City Park and Underground Parking Garage for Pittsburgh's Golden Triangle," prepared by Mitchell & Ritchey and George S. Richardson, consulting engineer, with the collaboration of Simonds & Simonds.

"Parking Park Study" focused on the area that would become known as Mellon Square, in the heart of the Golden Triangle. In the late 1940s the existing city block included a number of smaller-scale three- to four-story buildings, one twelve-story building, and a large parking lot, along with the Davis Theatre and the Peoples Gas Company. Trolley lines ran up and down both Sixth Avenue and Smithfield Street. The proposal claimed that the project would rehabilitate the area from the standpoint of business and real estate. The study also asserted that this project would fulfill "two long-felt needs of the Golden Triangle: spacious off-street parking capacity, and the ornamental and recreational values of a downtown park."[26] Here were contained the core ideas that would later give form to Mellon Square. Mitchell & Ritchey and Simonds & Simonds recommended a "stepped level" garage, widening of adjacent streets, introduction of stores and restaurants, and a sloping, terraced park.

Enter Edgar Kaufmann: Patron of Planning

Edgar Kaufmann, a businessman, founding ACCD member, and member of the Urban Redevelopment Authority, was keenly interested in reinventing Pittsburgh. [FIG. 26] He used Kaufmann's Department Store as a stage for new ideas, including celebrating Charles Lindbergh's trans-Atlantic flight in 1927 and commissioning a series of murals on the history of American trade by Boardman Robinson. He had long championed forward-thinking architecture; in 1935 his store exhibited architect Frank Lloyd Wright's model of "Broadacre City," a visionary plan for a decentralized community (the same year he commissioned Wright to design the famed residence Fallingwater). Two years later, Kaufmann commissioned Wright to design the department store's executive office. Wright created an elegant and warm interior, using swamp cypress plywood for geometrically-patterned wall paneling; he designed the furnishings, upholstery, and carpets as well.[27]

When visiting Pittsburgh for his 1935 exhibit at Kaufmann's, Wright observed that the city had wasted the potential of its rivers

FIG. 26
Architecture patron Edgar
Kaufmann Sr. commissioned
Frank Lloyd Wright to design his
corporate office at Kaufmann's
department store.

and hilly landscape, and so after World War II, Kaufmann engaged him to redesign Pittsburgh's then-derelict Point. Kaufmann chaired the ACCD committee charged with developing the plan for a substantial civic center to commemorate the Point's history, improve traffic flow, and provide a site for new office buildings. Wright responded to this new opportunity with a mega structure incorporating a sports arena, civic theater, opera house, aquarium, marina, gardens, retail spaces, parking areas, and fountain. Calling his 1947 design "Pittsburgh Point Park Coney Island in Automobile Scale," Wright described it as "a good time place, a people's place."[28] Even though his plan addressed the problem of the automobile with large-scale bridges, ramps, and parking garages, Wright was not successful in gaining the support of Pittsburgh's leaders for such a monumental undertaking.

But a parallel Kaufmann enterprise, also in 1947, was so well received that it did, in fact, shape the future of downtown Pittsburgh. To celebrate the seventy-fifth anniversary of Kaufmann's Department Store, Kaufmann commissioned Mitchell & Ritchey to envision Pittsburgh seventy-five years into the future. Mitchell & Ritchey consulted with Wallace Richards and Park Martin, and enlisted Simonds & Simonds to advance the concepts honed over the previous two years.[29] The team put forward futuristic design ideas that were displayed in an exhibit at the department store and a publication titled *Pittsburgh in Progress*.[30] [FIG. 27] The effort won a national award from the American Institute of Architects.

The team was clearly influenced by the French architect Le Corbusier's radical vision of destroying old cities and building anew at a vast scale, with towers studding an open landscape in an orderly array. The newly available view—looking down on the city from skyscrapers and airplanes—was a mighty force behind this new urban model, which Le Corbusier defined as the "Radiant City." As Carnegie Mellon University architecture librarian and archivist Martin Aurand explained,

FIG. 27
The public flocked to Kaufmann's
Pittsburgh in Progress exhibition.

When Pittsburghers looked out from their skyscrapers and down from their airplanes, they saw that what had appeared picturesque from oblique viewpoints on the surrounding hills now appeared chaotic and congested. *Life* magazine photographer Margaret Bourke-White took

FIG. 28
A rendering from Pittsburgh in Progress shows significant green spaces reaching from the Point to midtown, approximately where Mellon Square would be located.

indicting aerial photographs of Pittsburgh in 1938 and 1944. As Pittsburgh attacked its smoke problem, the view looked clearer and clearer, and the city looked worse and worse to the spectator.[31]

Pittsburgh in Progress is a fascinating Modernist approach to redesigning the city using its rivers and naturalistic features. Sketches showed bird's-eye views of a new Pittsburgh with tall skyscrapers set within a green landscape with decongestion and clean air and water. [FIG. 28] The approach reshaped the city to eliminate traffic hazards and parking problems, and to renew the heart of the community through specific projects at strategic locations throughout the city. This bold vision, expressed in graphic form, gained strong community and political support from leaders including Lawrence and Mellon.

Conflicting Design Approaches

As suggested by Mellon, precedents for the Mellon Square design concept were San Francisco's Union Square (1941) and Manhattan's Rockefeller Center (1939). The favored initial concept of the design team pushed beyond the defined park space onto three adjacent city

FIG. 29
With a 1949 model of Mellon
Square are Mayor Lawrence;
James McLain, the ACCD's
disbursing agent for Mellon Funds
and former planning director for
the Pittsburgh Regional Planning Association; and W. R. B.
Froehlich, chief planning engineer
for the PRPA and, in 1952, the first
executive director of the Pittsburgh Parking Authority.

streets, considered as park extensions. Opening
the first-floor levels of adjacent buildings directly
onto the park, the preliminary design created a
grand plaza that flowed to the lobby levels of
the William Penn Hotel, and the Alcoa and U.S.
Steel/Mellon Bank buildings one-half story above
the existing streets and sidewalks. Favoring the
pedestrian and the park experience, the plan left
Smithfield Street open, while closing the other
three streets or placing them underground.

Despite the team's encompassing concept, the scope of the project shifted back to an urban park contained by the city block and framed
by the adjacent streets. The design for a vibrant square, drawing on the
Rockefeller Center concept, evolved toward an "ice-skating rink at the level
of Smithfield Street" with an Eero Saarinen sculpture "backed by a two-
story restaurant, a la Rockefeller Center Plaza."[32] However this idea was
scuttled as the PPA added two more levels to the parking garage, which
shifted the concept to a simple platform with stairs rising from Smithfield
Street and retail spaces at street level. Following this development, Mitchell,
Ritchey, and Simonds reportedly retired to the Schenley Hotel bar, "cried a
little over their drinks, and went back to work."[33]

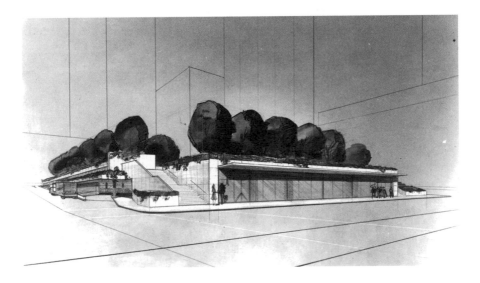

FIG. 30
This 1954 artist's sketch depicts Mellon Square as seen from the corner of Sixth Avenue and Smithfield Street.

Other Pittsburgh civic leaders influenced the design of Mellon Square as well. [FIG. 29] They included James McClain, who, as a former planning director for the RPA, had had a hand in the conception of the park idea, and who later acted for the ACCD as disbursing agent for Mellon funds going into the project; Robert Templeton, director of City Parks; and Robert B. Mulliken, project supervisor for the general contractor, H. K. Ferguson.

In its final form, Mellon Square was a composition that played symmetry against asymmetry, arranging passages, planting beds, and fountains to create layered spaces. The overall design responded to the downhill slope from William Penn Place to Smithfield Street with a plaza that tied surrounding buildings together in an island of calm—reinforced by dense plantings—above the confusion of busy streets. [FIG. 30] At its heart was the graceful display of water in active play and reflection, given a sparkling verdigris effect by small glazed tiles of beige, aqua, and copper tones, with a curving edge that seemed to float just above the paving. Framed by native trees and groundcovers, this oasis could be seen as an abstraction of a woodland glade. A dramatic water cascade along the grand staircase extended the oasis to the edge of the park, and made an inviting link to the one-story retail area along Smithfield Street.

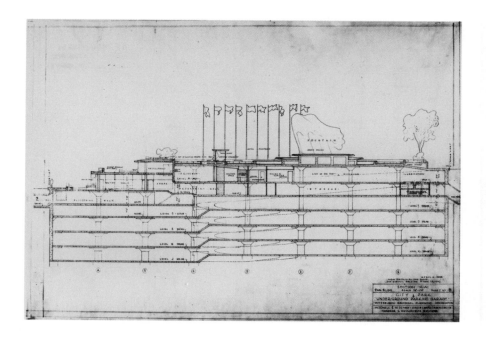

FIG. 31
A section of the Mellon Square
garage and park from "City & Park
Underground Parking Garage"
study, which was developed for
the Pittsburgh Regional Planning
Association in 1949.

Achieving Downtown's New Breathing Space

Funding for Mellon Square was secured in April 1949 when three Mellon
family foundations announced a $4 million gift to the City of Pittsburgh—
nearly 36 million in today's dollars.[34] The A. W. Mellon Education and
Charitable Trust committed $2 million to the project; the Sarah Mellon
Scaife Foundation $1 million; and the Richard King Mellon Foundation
$1 million. Of the total sum, $3.5 million was for purchasing the land and
the remainder was designated for the park landscape, later augmented
by an additional $300,000 in Mellon funding. The gift was made on the
condition that "the outdoor public park shall be maintained permanently
by the City of Pittsburgh and that no part of the property be used other
than for an exclusively public purpose."[35]

On April 23, 1949, Mayor Lawrence publicly unveiled plans for the $8 million combined park and six-story underground parking garage, including parking for more than one thousand cars, a row of shops facing Smithfield Street, and a plaza with plantings, fountains, and cascades. [FIG. 31] The $4 million garage portion of the project not financed by the Mellon family was to be paid for by public bonds and revenue from parking and retail rental space. Mayor Lawrence observed that the gift "will make it possible to break the congestion in the thickly built-up Triangle and give us a downtown breathing space and beauty spot that will be of enormous value."[36] Commenting on the city's transformation, *Fortune* magazine said "Pittsburgh is the test of industrialism everywhere to renew itself, to rebuild upon the gritty ruins of the past a society more equitable, more spacious, more in human scale."[37]

Plans for Mellon Square included demolishing sixteen commercial buildings, which spurred complaints of their loss from the city's tax rolls.[38] [FIG. 32] Critics also cited Pittsburgh's irregular and narrow street pattern and questioned the wisdom of setting a parking area within the business district, on the theory that a further concentration of vehicles would intensify traffic problems.[39] Despite these concerns, the reaction to the plan was overwhelmingly positive. Impacts were almost immediate, with construction of new office buildings surrounding the future square. With prospects of a park and parking garage, U.S. Steel and Alcoa both erected new office buildings at opposite corners, flanking the square's main entrance at William Penn Place. [FIG. 33]

In 1953 the city council named the block "Mellon Square." In September of that year, Mayor Lawrence turned over the first shovel of dirt in groundbreaking ceremonies. In his remarks at the ceremony, Mellon said, "this is the most important day in my life in Pittsburgh. To me this project is a very personal one."[40] As thousands of citizens assembled to watch the Pittsburgh Renaissance unfold, Mellon explained the purpose of the new park: "A quiet unspoiled haven of beauty, rest, and relaxation for individuals and small groups, open to the public at all times."[41] [FIG. 34]

Two years later, on October 18, 1955, the city celebrated Mellon Square's grand opening. The new plaza was dedicated to two brothers, Mellon's father Richard Beatty Mellon and his uncle Andrew

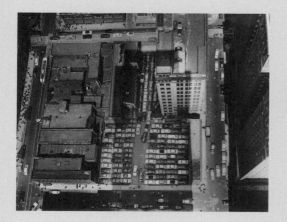

FIG. 32
A July 1951 aerial photograph of the city block shows some of the sixteen commercial buildings that were demolished.

FIG. 33
Retention of Alcoa was big news, as their new headquarters showcased

the artistic use of aluminum in almost every conceivable way, from waste receptacles to woven wall cladding.

FIG. 34
Ground was broken for Mellon Square on September 28, 1953.

Mellon. *Life* magazine photographer Margaret Bourke-White, who had
taken dramatic aerial photographs of smoke-shrouded Pittsburgh in
1936 and 1944, returned to Pittsburgh to capture Mellon and Mayor
Lawrence, the titans of the Pittsburgh Renaissance, in the resplendent
roof garden plaza.[42] From the outset, Mellon Square attracted local,
national, and international attention. It was, as Simonds wrote, "A civic
monument. Dedicated to the memory of two Mellon Brothers...planned
to epitomize also the dynamic and progressive spirit of Pittsburgh....
For the citizens a source of pride and lasting inspiration."[43]

3

Concepts and Ideas for Mellon Square, 1949–1955

Mellon had a steadily growing interest in developing a downtown business district, fed by the 1947 Pittsburgh in Progress exhibit at Kauffman's Department Store. He asked the RPA to study the feasibility of his vision for a park and underground parking garage.[1] In 1949 the RPA commissioned Mitchell & Ritchey to create an integrated complex for the Mellon enterprises that combined urban planning and design, architecture, and landscape architecture in the design of buildings, open space, and parking. The solution related modern architecture and existing buildings to a rooftop park above an underground parking garage. According to *Greater Pittsburgh* magazine, "On a Labor Day weekend at his home, James Mitchell drew up the basic concept of a park and underground garage. His sketch, which incidentally visualized the two new skyscrapers not yet planned, won approval of Mr. Mellon and two top aides, Wallace Richards and Park H. Martin."[2] They were given the job and immediately enlisted the landscape architects Simonds & Simonds to collaborate on the design.

Variations on the Park as Oasis

Early sketches that chronicle the evolution of design concepts for Mellon Square reside in the office archives of Simonds & Simonds (now EP&D). No Mitchell & Ritchey design sketches for the plaza have been uncovered. As often takes place in a design process, a variety of ideas were tested concurrently. The elevated position of the plaza over the garage provided opportunities to manipulate three-dimensional spaces with multiple levels connected by stairs and ramps. Common elements among the design concepts included a large, centrally positioned pool, memorials and monuments, a cafe or outdoor restaurant, and outdoor live animal displays. Several unsigned sketches have been clearly attributed to John O. Simonds by his successors as being in his hand and style.

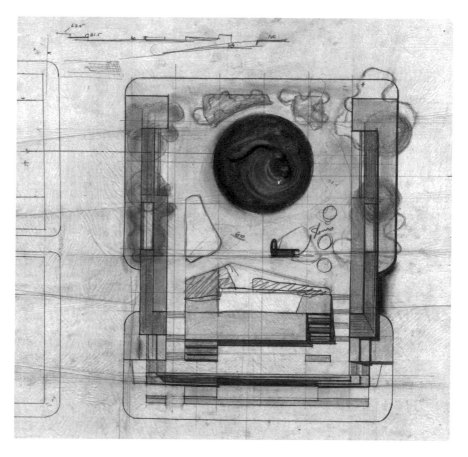

FIG. 35
Simonds's earliest known
conceptual sketch for Mellon
Square, dating to the 1940s, set
forth the oasis concept.

One of the first design sketches depicting the elevated platform, with steps rising from
the two Smithfield Street corners, is a chalk hard-
line drawing on tracing paper. [**FIG. 35**] It shows a large circular pool positioned toward the east near William Penn Place, with what appears to
be a three-piece sculptural element, in the style of the architect Eero
Saarinen, within it. Surrounding the pool is an open space framed by
free-flowing forms of lush vegetation within structured rectilinear edges.
A lightly sketched-in rounded trapezoid and three circles may also indicate planters. Occupying the western part of the plaza is a green space
or planter framed at both ends with stairs and cascading floral displays

leading to a secondary open space at a lower level, positioned as an anteroom to the main plaza. From this level, flights of stairs provide street access as they lead to the intersections of Smithfield Street with Sixth Avenue and Oliver Avenue. The edges along Sixth and Oliver provide access drives to the underground parking garage with rectangular planting beds above. The depth and multilevel intention of the design is seen through shadowing on the Oliver Avenue side and alluded to in a section study at the top of the drawing.

Variations on this early circular pool sketch were repeated as the design evolved. Here were foreshadowed key elements that would eventually define the ultimate form of Mellon Square. These include corner entrances, planter forms used to subdivide space and channel foot traffic, the central pool, cascading visual features, informal composition at the center framed by rectilinear elements providing separation from the surrounding city, and terraced plantings overhanging the garage entrances.

A second version of the sketch shows some similarities with more detail, including elevations and plant species. The framework and structure remain, with the pool surrounded by vegetated edges and steps leading to the street corners. [FIG. 36] A small rectangle is shown in the pool, which suggests a simplification of the sculptural element from the first concept sketch. The trapezoidal shape is used for a planting bed that separates the pool from the street, but with curving edge and bench to match the pool's arc. Together, the trio of planters provides an asymmetrical frame for the plaza's pool oasis. A long, narrow monument in the larger of the two rectangular planters gives an additional layer of separation between the pool area and the remaining space.

Notes on plant species show the direction of the firm's palette toward strongly contrasting foliage color and texture, such as the delicate silvery foliage of Russian olive (*Eleagnus angustifolia*) trees against the dark, toothy density of upright yew (*Taxus* × *media*) or the leathery, broad leaves of swamp bay magnolia (*Magnolia glauca*). Beyond these planters, the space is subdivided by rectilinear hedges with adjacent colored circles (which may indicate bedding plants). The length of the upper plaza's western edge is hedged with yews and eleven evenly spaced "Roses on Globes," set above evergreen bedding plants. Flanking staircases descend from the plaza to Smithfield Street, pausing midway at

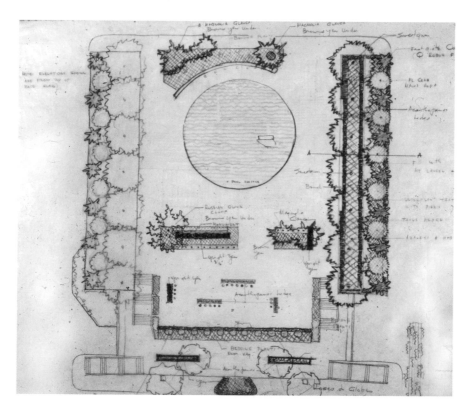

FIG. 36
This sketch began to develop
the surrounding planters
and introduced a monument wall.

a terrace level. Along these stairs, the concept of cascading floral displays again appears.

Additional planters placed along the street edge help to screen the plaza, using an interesting mix of deciduous and evergreen plants including trees, such as sweetgum (*Liquidambar styraciflua*), upright English oak (*Quercus robur* 'Fastigiata'), and crabapple (*Malus hopa*), with underplantings of andromeda (*Pieris japonica*), azaleas, and hybrid rhododendrons. Benches are placed along the edges of the planting beds for a close-up experience of these effusive, multi-toned plantings.

At the bottom of the drawing is a tantalizing abstract sketch. Shown in elevation, a basin rises above a waterline on an angled column or three supports, with two curved lines spouting from it in what could represent water sprays. [**FIG. 37**] This is the first record of what would become an iconic element of the final design for Mellon Square.

Through many renditions of possible design concepts, the design team discussed including live animal displays within the pool, such as flamingos, penguins, and sea lions, which were favored for their comical movements and expressions. Written notes from the discussion state, sea lions "can be enclosed by a three-foot rail....They can maneuver a steep slope and can make a direct rise of approximately two feet vertically which would indicate either a wide step or ramp design.... No trees or plants should be used in the active animal area. Concrete or stone slabs used for perches may be either wet or dry."[3] A more refined design study of the circular pool arrangement actually incorporated the idea of a live sea lion display. [FIG. 38] In the study, five circular platforms within the pool are elevated at various heights for sea lion interaction, and the pool is embedded within a grove of pin oak (*Quercus palustris*) in circular planters on a grid.

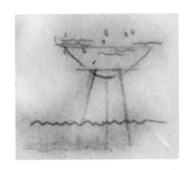

FIG. 37
A sketch affixed to the corner of figure two depicted a fountain bowl over a watery pool—the first emergence of what would become a signature element of the main pool.

Gaps in the grid of trees create openings that lead eastward to William Penn Place and to an open rectangular area on the plaza's west side. The planting composition, which defines the edge of this space, is also modified from the previous study. The study shows the edge plantings along the Sixth Avenue frontage in greater detail (and likely mirrored along Oliver Avenue), calling out plant selections that would have introduced sculptural forms through weeping beech (*Fagus sylvatica* 'Pendula') or hawthorne (*Crataegus* sp.), underplanted with finely textured blooming or berried shrubs, such as firethorn (*Pyracantha coccinea*). The sketch also introduces partially octagonal shapes overhanging the vehicular entrances to the underground garage, noted as planting beds.

Two sections accompanied the sea lion display sketch to further illustrate the design concept. This is the first appearance of the vertical angle, which would be ultimately used in the bench supports and drinking fountains. One section is taken through the planted edge of the plaza, showing a flowering crabapple (*Malus* sp.), holly (*Ilex* sp.), and

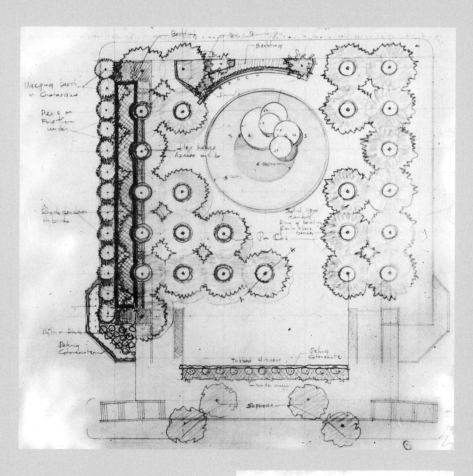

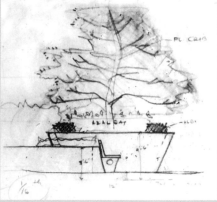

FIG. 38
Circular platforms for sea lion
perches were featured in this study.

FIG. 39
The angular motif that would
ultimately be applied to benches
and drinking fountains was
first depicted in a section that
accompanied figure four.

azalea (*Rhododendron* sp.) in a circular planter with a bench and planting area behind. [FIG. 39] The circular planter is 4.5 feet above the top of the slab of the parking garage, while the planter behind the bench is one foot lower. This reveals a heightened attention to detail given at this stage of the study to varying the volumes of the planters throughout the plaza.

From the Circular Pool to the Rectangular

From these early sketches of a circular pool, the order and geometric forms of Mellon Square evolved into a series of rectilinear forms. The pool became rectangular in shape, centered within the rhythmic and proportional rectangular forms of planters. [FIG. 40] In the center of the fountain are five small rectangular planting beds of an unspecified construction. Intersecting one side of the fountain is a memorial tower. It rises from groundcovers planted in what are labeled on the drawing as "architectural aluminum trays" with three "roses on frames" paralleling the tower on its east side. This is interesting both for the first use of aluminum in the concept development of Mellon Square and for the persistence of the floral form from earlier proposals, also repeated by "clematis on frames" in a nearby planting bed.

Planting beds front the plaza's north side, defining three entrances from William Penn Place. A long bench adjacent to the larger bed is positioned for a view of the fountain and its monumental memorial tower. Two additional memorials are shown as long, narrow walls situated to face the pool. [FIG. 41] Five rectangular planters are now placed on the opposite side of the fountain where previous sketches had located a large open space. The largest of these is turned perpendicularly, establishing a bold line of orientation, which will position the boxwood planter in the final design, channeling the primary flow of foot traffic between William Penn Place and Smithfield Street. West of the five rectangular planters is a restaurant opening onto a plaza-level dining terrace with the other side overlooking Smithfield Street. This is the first appearance of a restaurant in the conceptual development. In this iteration the garage entrances are located at the western edge along Smithfield Street.

A ramp works its way around the restaurant's north and west sides, giving access to the parking garage and the street level, also accessible by stair. Of particular note is a cascading fountain and floral

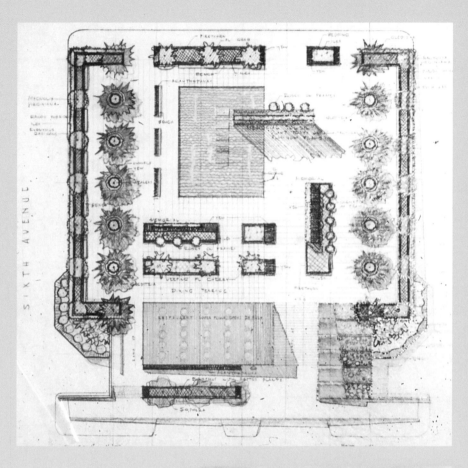

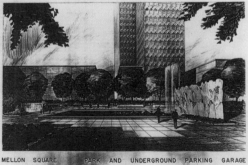

FIG. 40
Rectilinear forms dominated this study, which shows a cafe, dining terrace, and a cascade fountain at the corner of Smithfield Street and Oliver Avenue.

FIG. 41
A Mitchell & Ritchey perspective shows a monumental memorial sculpture perpendicular to the main pool.

display located southwest of the steps and restaurant—the first pairing of these elements, which will later become a signature of the final design.

While this concept is fairly porous from east to west, the north and south edges of the plaza are firmly separated from adjacent city streets by two layers of plantings. The dense screening ameliorates what could be a disconcerting change in grade along the sloping streets and creates the illusion of the plaza squarely confronting the facades on all four sides. Thornless honey locust (*Gleditsia triacanthos* var. *inermis*) trees are situated in circular planters to parallel the plaza-length planters along the Sixth Avenue and Oliver Avenue edges. A pattern of square block paving is shown throughout the upper level.

The Team's Final Proposal

After multiple revisions and refinements, Simonds & Simonds and Mitchell & Ritchey arrived at a design that closely resembles Mellon Square as it exists today. [FIG. 42] Models and sketches show a geometric design arranged with a series of rectangular planting beds and fountains on a plane of granite paving. A sizeable three-tiered fountain and pool is positioned off-center, and a large display of flagpoles is placed toward Sixth Avenue. Closer to the street edges are multiple tiered planting beds with deciduous trees and layers of understory. To either side of the retail frontage, which is set back from the street, are two stairways that provide entry to the midlevel restaurant and cafe area, and then turn ninety degrees to lead to the main plaza level. Cascading fountains and planting beds flank both sides of the stairways.

Throughout the design process, the members of the Mellon family offered their constructive criticism. The most striking input came from Sarah Mellon Scaife, R. K. Mellon's sister. [FIG. 43] On reviewing the preliminary design, she rejected the paving scheme of large granite rectangles. She told Simonds that she'd visited Venice and wanted smaller paving pieces like those in St. Mark's Square. He thought of triangles, Simonds later said, because the retail strip and garage entrances had to occupy three of the four edges, which required entrances at the corners and set up a pattern of diagonals.[4]

The design team's proposal for Mellon Square, "Revised Preliminary Study for Pittsburgh Garage," considered the Mellons' input

FIG. 42
This image presented the "City
Park and Underground Parking
Garage" to the public.

FIG. 43
Sarah Mellon Scaife, ca. 1940–1945.

and showcased the triangular paving pattern within a similar arrangement of rectangular pool and planting beds. [FIG. 44] The study further explored the idea of memorial walls, showing three "sculptural panels" arranged around the center of the Square. Similar to an earlier design, the largest sculptural panel intersects perpendicularly with the "Great Fountain Pool," with adjacent plant trays suspended on an architectural aluminum frame.

Toward Sixth Avenue, five honey locusts nested within circular planter benches provide a soft canopy of dappled light. This was an early use of the new thornless form of the honey locust tree, introduced in 1950 as a tolerant urban tree with an open canopy and fine texture giving a light shade. Along the street edge, a linear planting bed is crowned by seven littleleaf lindens (*Tilia cordata*) underplanted with English ivy (*Hedera helix*), and with rows of hybrid rhododendrons, firethorn, and a yew hedge. The same palette and composition is used along Oliver Avenue, establishing the densely planted frame for the plaza that would become an underpinning concept for edge plantings on these two frontages. Interestingly, the individual honey locust planters are not yet mirrored along the Oliver Avenue edge as they are in the final design. This plan reduces two water cascades to one, but at an enlarged scale.

The design of the edge along Smithfield Street is also substantially different from previous studies. A midlevel landing is accessed by stairs rising from the street. Between the overlook and the upper plaza level, five littleleaf linden trees in a large planter establish a fourth wall for the plaza that will remain a defining element in the final design. From the midlevel terrace, the steps continue up to the plaza, where benches line nearly all edges of the space, providing extensive seating next to rich plantings that are shaded by tree canopy.

Further refinements to this proposal resulted in the final design of Mellon Square. The "Pool Study for Mellon Square Park" made the main pool more rectangular and added eleven basins and a grid of water jets. [FIG. 45] The midlevel Smithfield Street terrace was eliminated and replaced with layers of vegetation above the retail frontage, now sheltered by a structural canopy. Elevations of street views illustrate the relationship of Mellon Square to downtown Pittsburgh with the plaza's scale, geometry, and proportion emerging from the ground plane into a series of complex forms with overhanging vegetation.

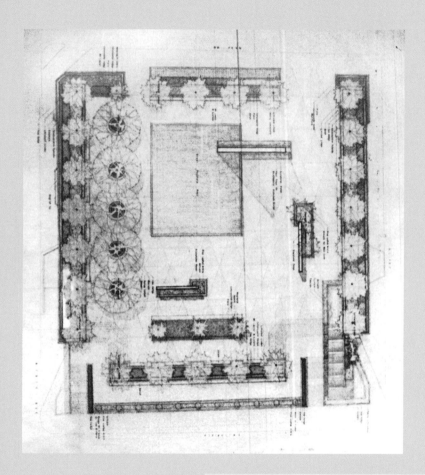

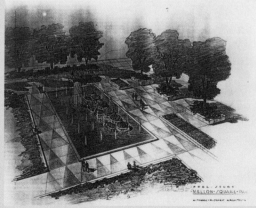

FIG. 44
Mitchell & Ritchey's "Revised
Preliminary Study for Pittsburgh
Garage" sketch from the early
1950s showed a triangular paving
pattern.

FIG. 45
This pool study showed eleven
basins and a grid of jets, with
the surrounding planter forms in
approximately their permanent
arrangement.

The City Explores its Options

With a solid foundation for a concept generated by Mitchell & Ritchey and Simonds & Simonds, and perhaps out of a combined motive of asserting ownership and due diligence, the City of Pittsburgh solicited additional designers for sketches and drawings of the proposed Square in April 1952. Howard B. Stewart, director of the Department of Parks and Recreation, contacted Ralph W. Olmstead of the Morrison-Knudsen Company, stating "the preliminary sketches [for Mellon Square] presented a very pretty picture but gave a rather vague idea of the actual design of the park...we wanted some means of expressing our preliminary ideas to you and finally decided that we would retain the services of Ralph E. Griswold and Associates, of Pittsburgh, as landscape architectural consultants, to work with us in setting up a design program..."[5]

Turning to Griswold was a saving grace. The landscape architect was highly regarded nationally and locally. [FIG. 46] A Rome Prize winner, Griswold had worked in the prominent offices of Bryant Fleming in Buffalo and A. D. Taylor in Cleveland before moving to Pittsburgh in 1927 to work with Clarence Stein and Henry Wright on the planned community of Chatham Village. From 1934–1945 he was superintendent of the Pittsburgh Bureau of Parks, driving a renewal and expansion of the parks system by leading a dizzying array of improvements funded through New Deal programs. After leaving the city's employ, he founded the firm Griswold, Winters, Swain and Mullin in 1948. GWSM's portfolio included significant projects ranging from the American Cemetery at Anzio, Italy, to Pittsburgh's Zoo and Point State Park (in collaboration with Clarke + Rapuano).

FIG. 46
Ralph E. Griswold, ca. 1954.

Stewart's letter to Olmstead presented Griswold's program, which was fortunately well aligned with the Mitchell & Ritchey and Simonds & Simonds concepts. Designs were requested for "three different schemes, one to include a restaurant above the shops opening onto the park level, another featuring an ornamental fountain using aluminum and stainless steel, and a third showing a fountain in which seals, penguins or flamingoes may be displayed when the season permits. All three of these ideas have been proposed by individuals vitally interested in the design of the park."[6]

Undoubtedly due to Griswold's influence, the city also specified that the design "must belong distinctly to this spot" and "not be transferred appropriately to any other location."[7] To accomplish this, the city noted that the design should relate to local downtown climatic and atmospheric conditions; sun and adjacent building orientation; historic, economic, and social traditions; and local habits and customs. The design should also include "cost of maintenance, durability and permanence of structural and plant materials, immediate effect of plant material in relation to ultimate effect, choice of structural materials in color relations to plant materials, and design appeal as a major attraction."[8] Practical features included ample surface drainage, heated snow-melting pedestrian walks, automatic irrigation system, "drinking fountains, caretaker's headquarters and equipment storage, and lighting—using underground cable and concealed lighting techniques—no light poles" using the four-foot difference in elevation between the top concrete slab of the underground parking garage and the "maximum four foot depth of soil required for trees."[9] The city's letter also stressed that the schemes should not duplicate the design of the proposed Point State Park or Gateway Center. Preferred schemes would use paving, planted areas, and trees, without using turf grass, which invites "loafers, sun bathers, and derelicts who will discourage the intended use by guests and workers from the surrounding office buildings and hotels."[10]

Responding within days to the city's request, Olmstead cautioned that the design with a restaurant above the shops "may be a difficulty since the grant for the park requires that the entire level above the garage be developed into a park."[11] Olmstead also warned against using ornamental metals for a fountain, due to the weight of the structure, which would have to be distributed to columns, and he did not favor using the fountain for seals, penguins, or flamingoes.

Whether Morrison-Knudsen produced or submitted any concept sketches for Mellon Square is unknown. The firm did, however, join the design team of Mitchell & Ritchey and Simonds & Simonds two years later for the construction of Mellon Square.

Building the Square

Once the complete funding package was securely in place (including $4 million in public bonds for garage construction in addition to the Mellon's $4 million for the plaza), the city moved forward with the final design for Mellon Square. The firms of Mitchell & Ritchey and Simonds & Simonds were asked to prepare construction documents. The project became Mitchell & Ritchey's first major architectural contribution to the physical rebuilding of Pittsburgh.

Site work at Mellon Square began in 1952, shortly after the city formally authorized the parking garage portion of the project and leased the subsurface rights to the PPA, who then subleased the underground area to a private corporation. The corporation, a combination of the Morrison-Knudsen Company and the H. K. Ferguson Company, agreed to design, build, and operate the garage at no cost to the city or the PPA. Demolition of the first structures at Mellon Square commenced on July 7, 1952, and continued for an entire year. During excavation, enough material was hauled out to fill 540 boxcars and, later, enough concrete was poured into the hole to fill 90 boxcars.[12]

Despite fears of lost tax revenue with the demolished structures, a Pennsylvania Economy League report showed a net loss in assessed value of buildings removed for Mellon Square of $2,459,750 in the block, as compared with a net gain of $15,972,885 in the area immediately surrounding it. Between 1953 and 1955 the assessed value rose to over $20,000,000.

After land acquisition, approximately $340,000 remained of the total $4,000,000 gift from the Trustees of the A. W. Mellon Educational and Charitable Trust, the Sarah Mellon Scaife Foundation, and the Richard King Mellon Foundation. The estimate for the construction, landscaping, and decoration of the plaza amounted to approximately $650,000. In August 1954 the three foundations consented to contribute the additional funds. The executive committee of the ACCD agreed to act as disbursing agent of the construction funds and to assume the obligation of being the contracting agent.

Construction Moves Forward

In June 1954 a plan of the park surface showing elevations of parapets, planting pocket walls, and granite shelves was issued by Mitchell & Ritchey and Simonds & Simonds. Construction specifications for the park were submitted and approved in August 1954. In September the Morrison-Knudsen Company, the H. K. Ferguson Company, and the ACCD signed a contract for the construction of Mellon Square, which began on October 6, 1954. [FIG. 47]

Throughout planning and construction, periodic meetings with design and construction professionals resulted in slight design refinements. For example, the H. K. Ferguson Company was unable to obtain gravel of a color suitable to architects Mitchell & Ritchey to cover the roof of the shops on Smithfield Street. Instead, the architects recommended accepting a substitution of #2 limestone chips.

The garage opened for limited public parking on January 3, 1955, though it did not open fully until May of that same year. Constructed with six underground parking levels, the garage had circular ramps, a straight ramp, 8,748 square feet of commercial space, 8-foot floor-to-ceiling height, 6.5 foot maximum clearance, a reversible escalator, an elevator, and three stairways. Each parking floor was decorated in an individual identifying color, which was matched by the color of the parking tickets and coordinated with the pool tile colors: sea green, gray, coral, terra cotta, yellow, and light blue. Parking garage attendants had access to amenities including dressing and shower rooms. At the lowest level of the garage were relief vents that allowed underground water to flood the level at times of high water to equalize pressure and hold the building down. [FIG. 48]

A PPA survey conducted soon after the opening showed that 37 percent of the parkers using Mellon Square during the weekdays were shoppers, and the figure jumped to 78 percent on Saturdays, reflecting the vibrant downtown retail market of that era. By mid-October 1955 between 1,700 and 1,800 automobiles filled Mellon Square Garage to capacity daily.

In February 1955 the park was nearly ready to receive plantings. Vegetation was selected by Simonds & Simonds and the city horticulturalist, Frank Curto, from nurseries across the country, including

FIG. 47
Onlookers observed the laying of
rebar during construction.

FIG. 48
The parking garage was designed
with relief vents, allowing water to
flood the lowest level at times of
high water to equalize pressure.

FIG. 49
Thornless honey locusts, then new
to the trade, were among the largest
trees to be planted.

Illinois, Ohio, Pennsylvania, New York, Virginia, New Jersey, and Maryland. Laborers readied the planting boxes by placing gravel, straw, and a topsoil mixture. The first tree was planted in Mellon Square on February 28. That same day six metal tree boxes were eliminated from the park plan because a revised rooting plan indicated a change from surface-rooted littleleaf linden to deep-rooted sweet gum. In May 1955 landscape contractor John Eisler and subcontractor Louis Hahn & Son agreed to substitute, at no extra cost, 1,296 plants of the "superior" "Hahn's English Ivy Shamrock" for the Baltic ivy (Hedera helix baltica) originally specified (which may have proven more resilient in the end).[13] Planting continued into the spring and concluded in June 1955.

The donors had specified that the park "should have a 'finished' appearance from the very beginning," requiring the selection of large trees.[14] [FIG. 49] The largest to be planted were the honey locust, sweetgum, and littleleaf linden. Rare trees included five Waterer Scots Pine (Pinus sylvestris 'Watereri') and a Japanese pagoda tree. Also in the park were sweetbay magnolias noted for their unusual fragrance, beeches clipped to form a foliage wall along William Penn Place, more than 250 azaleas and hybrid rhododendron, red chokeberry (Aronia arbutifolia), nearly 1,000 assorted evergreen shrubs, and 22,000 ivy plants in several varieties (see complete plant list in the Appendix, p. 152.). [FIG. 50]

Plant materials were chosen for the overall design as well as the "worst possible environmental conditions" including air pollution, heat, and amount of light. Contractors were required to use only those selected plants. The trees were set in steel boxes to prevent root growth from penetrating the roof surface below. Planter soil depths ranged from a minimum of fourteen inches to a maximum of four feet. Six inches

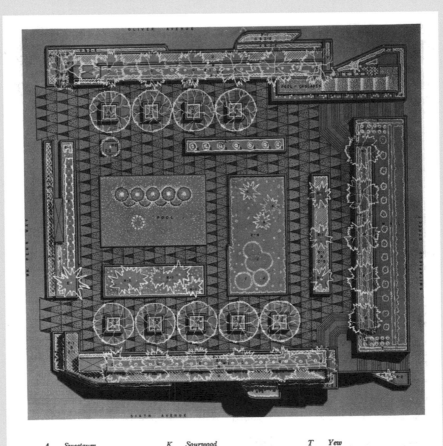

A	Sweetgum	K	Sourwood	T	Yew
B-1	Zumi Crab	L	Azalea	U	Scarlet Firethorn
B-2	Columnar Crab	M	Maries Doublefile Viburnum	V	Purpleleaf Euonymus
B-3	Eley Purple Crab	N	Red Chokeberry	W-1	Pink Rhododendron
C	Littleleaf Linden	O	Wintergreen Barberry	W-2	Red Rhododendron
D	Honeylocust	P-1	Roundleaf Japanese Holly	W-3	Boursault Rhododendron
E	Japanese Pagodatree	P-2	Stokes Holly	Y	Pachysandra
F	European Beech	P-3	Convexleaf Holly	Z-1	English Ivy
G	Franklinia	Q	Ibolium Privet	Z-2	Baltic Ivy
H-1	Sweetbay Magnolia	R-1	Japanese Pieris	Z-3	Miniature Ivy
H-2	Saucer Magnolia	R-2	Mountain Pieris	Z-4	Hahn's Maple Queen Ivy
J	Waterer Scotch Pine	S	Box	Z-5	Hahn's Green Ripple Ivy

FIG. 50
Simonds & Simonds produced a
lushly varied planting design, with
bold strokes of color from mass
plantings of azalea, rhododendron,
and pieris.

FIGS. 51 AND 52
Matthews Company Foundry
cast the nine bronze basins in
Pittsburgh, reportedly the largest
ever made as a single casting.

of gravel was provided for drainage, followed by a four-inch layer of compacted straw and composted mushroom soil. Ericaceous plants were pocket-planted in oversized holes filled with pure Canadian peat moss. Two large and two small planters were reserved for floral displays marked "By Other" on the planting plan, and were filled by the Department of Parks and Recreation with customary spring bulbs, summer annuals, and chrysanthemums in mid-October 1955. Large tropical foliage plants such as croton and hibiscus were planted in the planter that was also used for holiday display.

Plants were well protected. They were regularly fertilized and sprayed with an anti-desiccant for winter protection. In 1960 signs identifying vegetation were placed in each planting bed. To guard the plants from theft and vandalism, two attendants were on duty in daylight hours—and at least one was there around the clock. Assistant Police Superintendent Lawrence J. Maloney ordered all uniformed policemen in the area to "keep a vigil."[15]

Before construction was complete, the mechanical systems in the park were field tested for functionality and appearance, and final issues were resolved. Architects, engineers, contractors, and the ACCD reviewed lighting and hydraulics, adjusting levels as needed. Between April and June 1955, frequent inspections revealed a number of delays with the large bronze basins for the main fountain, which had been cast at the Matthews Company Foundry. Touted as the largest bronze basins in the world at 3,500 pounds each, their manufacturing defects included

FIG. 53
Gold leaf ensured legibility for the plaque's small type, which read "Their industrial leadership, civic spirit and philanthropy advanced immeasurably the welfare of the community."

pitting on the outside surface, inconsistent weathering of the patina, and an incorrect lip profile that did not match specifications. Water tests in June also demonstrated that water flowed unevenly from the basins and created turbulence. The Matthews Company made minor adjustments to the original design in order to achieve the proper water flow and resolved the issue in time for installation at Mellon Square. Basins of that size can never be duplicated because government regulations now limit foundries to pouring no more than 1,500 pounds at a time for safety reasons. [FIGS. 51 AND 52]

Other refinements were also essential before the park was opened. An inspection of the aluminum handrail revealed that it failed to meet the architectural details specified, and the holes in the granite were mislocated and improperly drilled. The H. K. Ferguson Company recommended filling the holes with patching compound, colored to match the stone, and the ACCD later approved this remedy. The design for the memorial plaque honoring Richard Beatty Mellon and Andrew Mellon also needed refinement. In June 1955 Park H. Martin, director of the ACCD, expressed concern that the small letters were almost illegible. Following approval from the architects, the H. K. Ferguson Company applied black paint and gold leaf to the incised lettering. [FIG. 53]

On June 21, 1955, representatives of the Department of Parks and Recreation and the ACCD inspected the entire site, finding Mellon Square to be in accordance with the plans and specifications. The Department of Parks and Recreation assumed maintenance responsibility for the park as of June 22.

On July 15 the last bronze basin for the main fountain was put into place. In August ring lights at the base of the main pool were lowered into the water so that they were completely submerged below the surface. Final inspection of the plaza occurred at ten o'clock in the morning on October 7. On the dedication date, October 18, 1955, Martin certified that the Morrison-Knudsen Company and the H. K. Ferguson Company completed the construction in accordance with the plans and specifications and to the satisfaction of the ACCD.

In preparation for the grand opening, numerous newspaper articles reflected on the construction process and unique features of Mellon Square. Waterproofing was one of the most exacting tasks. Some two hundred separate drains had to be separately waterproofed for the surface drainage system, sprinkler system, and circulation systems for the fountains. Warren-Ehret Company, in consultation with Koppers, engineered the intricate roofing job:

> The waterproofing treatment was applied over the entire area. Of the park proper, in five plies of tar-impregnated fabric and six alternating layers of tar pitch. In addition, under the fountain and cascade areas, and under all tree baskets and planters, two extra plies of fabric and a layer of waterproof concrete were applied. For the roofing over the storerooms, six of which front the west side of the square, four plies of tar-treated felt were alternated with five layers of pitch....[16]

All too soon, inadequate waterproofing technology (although the best available at the time), ill-maintained drains, and microclimate-challenged plantings would prove to be Mellon Square's greatest technical challenges. What was intended to be a delightfully refreshing space did not meet the funders' expectations due to the city's failure to provide adequate maintenance, costing Pittsburgh years of prolonged issues and millions of dollars in eventual renovations.

4

Elevating the Square: Platform, Trees, and Water

FIG. 54
Henri Marcus Moran, *View of Mellon Square—Looking North*, ca. 1955, Gouache on board, 15 x 19 in.

Pittsburgh's urban redevelopment took form in the mid-1950s with the completion of Mellon Square, adding a lynchpin greenspace to the urban fabric: a rooftop garden that functions on multiple tangible and intangible levels. As designed and constructed, it is an urban oasis offering a rich variety of visual and sensory perceptions. Mellon Square provides for daily and special event uses, for both casual and organized enjoyment. Simonds and his collaborators created a powerfully original landscape architecture and urban design solution in response to significant historic buildings, while also complimenting those newly constructed Modernist structures. They placed nature in high relief against the building-lined streets of downtown. [**FIG. 54**] Mellon Square evoked both a new and sophisticated image of the city while elevating the ideal for site-specific urban design solutions.

Achieving such a park required a multifaceted approach. As John O. Simonds said in a 1973 article for *Landscape Architecture*, "the architects and their collaborating landscape architects set about as a team in search of the highest concept for such a contemporary urban park. They soon found that such a park could not be conceived in terms of a single concept alone, but must be considered rather from many points of view and must be at once an expression of many things—some aesthetic, some idealistic, and some mundanely practical."[1] Simonds further defined these conceptual facets, writing:

> The Square must be:
>
> A *platform*. [FIG. 55] For structurally the park would be in effect a sloping deck atop a five-story underground garage. On this concrete slab, as on a vast tray, must be placed all elements—the fountains, cascades, pavement, benches, and all trees and other plants in shallow boxes, tubs, and bins.
>
> A *structure*. All loads imposed on the park surface must be carried by columns through the entire structure to the footings spaced out on the floor of a prehistoric stream bed some sixty feet below. Weights and positions were critical. The park plan must in many ways be a diagram of optimum maximum column loadings. The fountain base was precisely placed to span a column grouping, and each major tree was centered squarely on a prelocated column cap.
>
> An *island*. [FIG. 56] The Square is surrounded by and cut off from the rest of the city by four streams of heavy traffic. This insular character dictated the need of strong plan forms at the perimeter to withstand the traffic's force of erosion. It set the park approaches at those points where pedestrians could best and most safely cross the streets. It suggested that the park surface be lifted up above the streets to lose by elevation and sight lines the street and traffic confusion.
>
> A *space*. Perhaps the greatest value of Mellon Square is that here among the surrounding city canyons is at last a significance space. Again, by the fact of the lifting up, the apparent limits of this volume were extended beyond the screened-off streets to the facades of the flanking buildings on all sides. This civic space was expanded, modulated, and articulated by all means at the architects' command. [FIG. 57]

FIG. 55
The "vast tray" of the plaza's
platform was apparent in this
photograph of the southwest
corner of the park.

FIG. 56
Mellon Square was well-defined
as an island, set apart from
surrounding traffic.

A focal center. Two new office towers, for U.S. Steel and for Alcoa, were proposed at the time of, and as a result of, the Square's inception. It was evident that the park space should function as a focal point for these and the existing structures which would surround it on four sides. It must relate structures and space into one harmonious unity. It must also serve, for each building seen from within the park, as an appropriate foreground.

A civic monument. Dedicated to the memory of two Mellon brothers, it was planned to epitomize also the dynamic and progressive spirit of Pittsburgh. In concept and form it must bespeak high idealism. It must be for the citizens a source of pride and lasting inspiration.

A gathering place. [FIG. 58] A city square is for people. It must attract and accommodate crowds. It is a meeting place. It is a passing-through place. It is a waiting-for and greeting place. It is a stay-awhile and relaxing place. It must be human in scale and human in its appeal.

An oasis. In the oppressive and barren cityscape a park must be—perhaps most of all—a cool refreshing oasis. In contrast with the sharp building profiles and the hard surface and dull hues of pavement, building stone, and brick, it must give the welcome relief of foliage, shade, splashing water, flowers, and bright color. Like the oasis that it is, the urban park must be a place of pure delight—an inviting refreshing environment."[2]

Simonds's elaborate and precise statement of design intent reveals his deep understanding and aspirational quest for this rare, highly articulated urban park that sits on a rooftop and is nested in a dynamic and changing downtown. As the project evolved, its primary financial supporters, the A. W. Mellon Education and Charitable Trust, the Sarah Mellon Scaife Foundation, and the Richard King Mellon Foundation, also made their preferences clear. They desired a passive park that served as a breathing space in the dense downtown. The Mellons wanted "a quiet unspoiled haven of beauty, rest, and relaxation for individuals and small groups, open to the public at all times."[3]

FIG. 57
Lifting the plaza above the street
extended the civic space to the
facades of surrounding buildings.

FIG. 58
Mellon Square's success as a
"gathering place" was captured in
this photograph from the Simonds
collection, ca. 1956.

Key Design Elements

The Mellon Square design evolved as a layered composition with a concentric sequence of elements. [FIG. 59] The heart of the plaza, with its graceful, light-toned water display of the rectangular pool with nine large bronze basins, expressed the dual elements of active and reflective water. It was a modern, graceful, crisp, yet intricately detailed water feature that appeared as a series of overlapping water and structural elements. Tile cladding was arranged in a triangular mosaic pattern to produce a watery, verdigris effect.[4] The shape of the main fountain was simple in plan but complex in profile, with a curving cantilevered coping. [FIG. 60] A choreographed water display with a grid of low-spraying jets and a dominant high-spraying asymmetrical main jet provided an animated focal point of constant change throughout the day and evening. [FIG. 61]

The heart of the plaza's interior composition was the central fountain pool, paving, and framing planters. In the abstract, the fountain itself could be interpreted as a series of springs spilling into a pool in a forest glade. Surrounding the central pool, positioned in bright sunlight, planters supported trees and groundcovers on two sides, with trimmed trees as a narrow green wall on a third side, and flowers with evergreen shrubs on the fourth. The native magnolias and craggy pines "reinforce the sense of abstracted hyper-forest. This type of abstraction may draw on the Japanese and Chinese design styles, familiar to Simonds, where individual plants and plant groupings often symbolize a broader wilderness."[5]

The fountain cascade, addressing the grade change at the corner of Oliver and Smithfield Streets, extended these natural ideas to the urban edge. Water rose from a trio of jets in the upper basin and fed the series of five cascading tile-surfaced trays on its way to the street-level receiving pool. Shallow planters at each cascade level provided color and a contrasting soft texture to the dramatic flight of granite steps. The sound, motion, and reflected light from the water, along with these bright plantings, invited pedestrians to the plaza level. [FIG. 62]

Surrounding the central fountain was a second tier of granite-faced waist-high planter boxes. In these individual planter boxes and aligned with the top of the steps, the canopies of honey locust and

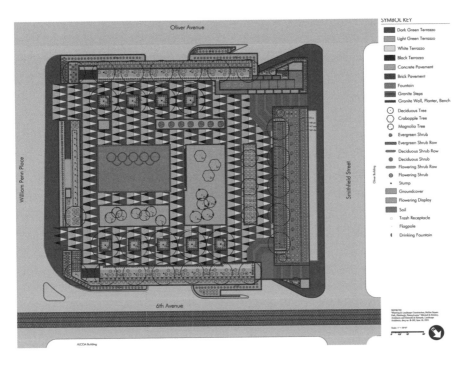

SYMBOL KEY

Dark Green Terrazzo
Light Green Terrazzo
White Terrazzo
Black Terrazzo
Concrete Pavement
Brick Pavement
Fountain
Granite Steps
Granite Wall, Planter, Bench
Deciduous Tree
Crabapple Tree
Magnolia Tree
Evergreen Shrub
Evergreen Shrub Row
Deciduous Shrub Row
Deciduous Shrub
Flowering Shrub Row
Flowering Shrub
Stump
Groundcover
Flowering Display
Soil
Trash Receptacle
Flagpole
Drinking Fountain

FIG. 59
"1959 Period Plan—As Built."

crabapple trees provided scale and a woodland quality of alternating bright, filtered, and shaded light.

The third tier of rough terrazzo paving, planter walls, and profuse plantings formed the final spatial container. From within Mellon Square these planters mediated with building facades to form a tree-lined frame at eye level and above with the "Iridian" granite, understory plantings, and canopy of linden and sweet gum.

A final element, the planting bed above the Smithfield Street facade, inaccessible to pedestrians, served as a visual amenity to surrounding high-rise buildings, particularly the Oliver Building directly across the street.[6] The flowering shrub plantings of the original design related to the understory plantings within the tree planters.

Within each of these sequential tiers of planters, plantings, and integrated benches, the strong pattern and four-color arrangement of the triangular paving unified the composition, with paving extended

FIG. 60
Water lapping at the main fountain's curved coping induced the sense of a spring-fed pool.

FIG. 61
Pedestrians were enticed to the plaza level by the fountain's sound, motion, and reflected light.

opposite:
FIG. 62
The elegant fountain display was choreographed so each movement would last a minimum of five minutes, with periods of calm for a subtle effect.

FIG. 63
The triangular paving was exceptionally striking at night, highlighted by the plaza's extensive yet subtle lighting.

onto the perimeter sidewalk at William Penn Place, inviting pedestrians and signaling the detail to be found within. [FIG. 63]

Once the signature triangular paving was selected, Simonds wanted to use terrazzo. He turned to his brother, as he frequently did, to develop the solution.[7]

Normally used indoors, typical polished terrazzo would create a slippery, hazardous surface when wet. Philip Simonds reasoned that if the terrazzo was not cut or polished, then it could be used as a "rustic" material. As former colleague, landscape architect Bob Vukich has recalled, "Phil was always asking what other way it can be done—he was innovative."[8] Working with local contractor Patrizio Mosaic, Philip developed the construction details with colored marble chips and colored mortar in four combinations divided by the traditional bronze strips. As a unique pavement with historic origins in Mellon Square, "Rustic Terrazzo" was later adopted as the City of Pittsburgh's preferred design standard for downtown sidewalks.

Other innovations included the placement of heating pipes under the paving to melt snow, and trash receptacles buried at the inside corners of several tree planter boxes. While these were well integrated into the park landscape, they proved a maintenance challenge.

Meeting the Street and Beyond

The Smithfield Street frontage provided storefront linkages between Mellon Square and the bustle of contiguous city streets. Retail stores in the newly created commercial spaces along Smithfield included a hosiery shop, a candy store, and a bakery. In time, these businesses would be replaced with service-oriented tenants, such as the Port Authority of Allegheny County, and the uniform glass fronts, stainless steel frames, and consistent signage would be modified repeatedly. By the 1990s this frontage evolved into an unappealing stretch of sidewalk beneath a dark overhang with little interest to passersby, and no services related to park use.

"Mellon Square is a fine architecture-viewing platform," according to the Pittsburgh History & Landmarks Foundation (PHLF), which describes the wealth of structures surrounding the plaza (and throughout downtown) in walking tours and guidebooks.[9] The buildings

surrounding Mellon Square presented a cyclo-
ramic view of the city's architectural and social
history, while the range of architectural character and scale contributed to the rich experience
of the plaza. In particular, the airy steeple of
the Smithfield United Church gave welcome
relief to the otherwise dense skyline, while the
modern patterns of the Alcoa building set up
a symphonic dialogue with Mellon Square's
triangular pavement. [FIGS. 64 AND 65] Other
buildings include the William Penn Hotel (now
Omni William Penn Hotel), Union Arcade (now
Union Trust Building), U.S. Steel/Mellon Bank
Building (now 525 William Penn Place), Mellon
Bank Building (now PNC Service Center),
Henry W. Oliver Building, and Kaufmann &
Baer Co. Department Store (now Heinz 57
Center). [FIGS. 66–71]

Workers and visitors in neighboring
buildings looked down on a pleasingly patterned
open space, animated by a diversity of materials, textures, foliage, choreography of water
displays, and people. The scale of the elements
also worked from within the Square, offering
both bold and soothing delight for the eye in
the colors and patterns of materials and plantings. [FIG. 72] Landscape architect Patricia M.
O'Donnell, principal author of the 2009 plan to
restore Mellon Square, summarized this effect:

FIG. 64
Pittsburgh's architectural history
is on view from Mellon Square,
including Henry Hornbostel's
Smithfield United Church with its
aluminum openwork spire, 1925–26.

FIG. 65
Regional Enterprise Tower

This interplay of superior and inferior views represents a
highly important part of the design. Combined with the rep-
etition and interaction of forms and patterns of the Square
with the Oliver Building, Omni William Penn Hotel, Alcoa
Building, and U.S. Steel Building, views to and from the
Square are quite visually engaging. The triangular pavement

FIG. 66
Omni William Penn Hotel

FIG. 67
Union Trust Building

FIG. 68
U.S. Steel/Mellon Bank Building

FIG. 69
Former Mellon Bank Building

FIG. 70
Henry W. Oliver Building

FIG. 71
Former Kaufmann & Baer Co.
Department Store

FIG. 72
Mellon Square succeeded at both
scales—the dramatic aerial view,
and the intimate human scale.

juxtaposed with the rhythmic proportions of the adjacent building fenestration and detailing creates an integrated four-sided composition of building and landscape.[10]

From the surrounding streets, the vertical and horizontal planes that transitioned the change in grade and formed the outer tier of planters and planter walls lent the streetscape a human scale and tactile quality that served as the precursor and invitation to pedestrians, an enticement to the interior of this green, patterned urban island. By today's definition one can suggest that Mellon Square was Pittsburgh's original green roof. It was undoubtedly the product of a harmonious relationship between architect and landscape architect. Simonds had a clear and typically humble approach, as he described in an address to fellow landscape architects: "Take the blame and give away the credit. If things go wrong—if things go right—this is the key to successful collaboration."[11]

O'Donnell further observes, "This early urban reimaging project is thoroughly and well-recorded as a true collaboration led by design professionals with donor, civic leader, and city input. Simonds & Simonds and Mitchell & Ritchey carried out this landmark project together.... However, the early sketches by Simonds document his leadership in giving form to the uniqueness, intricacies, and innovations of Mellon Square."[12]

5

Lifecycles

The goal of Mellon Square was lofty. At the groundbreaking ceremony on September 28, 1953, Mayor Lawrence remarked, "This will be the very center, the heart, of the new Pittsburgh."[1] At the dedication ceremony two years later Richard King Mellon presented the park to the city as a gift from his family, and Mayor Lawrence accepted it on behalf of the residents of Pittsburgh. [FIG. 73] The *Pittsburgh Post-Gazette* reported that Mellon Square was "dedicated not only as a symbol of Pittsburgh's progress but as the city's first memorial to two of its greatest benefactors—the late Andrew W. Mellon and his brother, the late Richard B. Mellon."[2] Other speakers at the ceremony included Park H. Martin and Leland Hazard, both associated with the ACCD. Across the street, the marquee of the William Penn Hotel crowed, "Behold Beautiful Mellon Square Park, America's Most Beautiful Civic Plaza."

The ACCD prepared general information on Mellon Square for the dedication ceremony stating, "In the magnificence of its design and finish, Mellon Square Park is the finest in America. It is also unique in having no pedestrian walks crossing vehicle entrances and exits, and in having an integral commercial section."[3] The description went on to detail: "the black marble chips for the walks are from Belgium, Domestic Gray chips from Italy, Botticino (Green) from Italy, and Cardiff Green from Maryland; the cascades and large fountain pools entirely lined with weatherproof faience mosaic ceramic tile from Zanesville, Ohio; and the fountain comprising 11 varying colors in pattern in the tiles of the main pool, and three colors in the cascades."[4] Other structural features highlighted by the ACCD included aluminum handrails and light louvers, two drinking fountains, four aluminum waste receptacles inset in repositories within the tree planter boxes, lead-coated, copper-lined gutters with aluminum grating for drainage, and nineteen flagpole bases.

FIG. 73
Opening day, October 16, 1955,
was cause for great celebration.

Two weeks later the city council passed a resolution to formally name the block "Mellon Square." Multiple newspapers published
articles heralding the project. One read, "No better investment has been
made in Pittsburgh and its central business district than the $7,800,000
that has gone into construction of Mellon Square Park and Mellon
Square Garage, Inc., beneath it."[5] Mellon Square was also touted as the
"only park underground garage structure of its type in the United States
that contains a shopping center."[6] [FIG. 74]

Once opened to the public, the professional press gave serious attention to the project and its impacts. "A Green Square in the
Golden Triangle" was the tag line for the December 1955 cover article
in *Charette* (the "Official Publication of the Pennsylvania Society of
Architects, Pittsburgh Chapter, AIA, and the Pittsburgh Architectural

Club"). In the article John Mauro, editor of
Greater Pittsburgh magazine, proclaimed the
acre of greenery to be without peer in the nation.
Mauro quotes Mitchell as saying, "Only the finest of materials were used. The three Mellon
foundations were determined that Pittsburgh
should have the best. That was uppermost in
our minds."[7]

Peer acclaim was also forthcoming.
Just after the dedication, Ralph E. Griswold
wrote letters of praise to most of the key individuals involved. To Mellon, Griswold wrote,

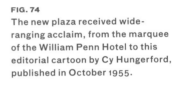

FIG. 74
The new plaza received wide-
ranging acclaim, from the marquee
of the William Penn Hotel to this
editorial cartoon by Cy Hungerford,
published in October 1955.

> This morning, for the first time since I
> came to this city 28 years ago, I was
> inspired by the sight that greeted me
> when I arrived in downtown Pittsburgh. As I walked through
> Mellon Square from the Northeast to the Southwest corners
> a beam of sunlight streamed down between the buildings
> spotlighting the fountain at the head of the cascade....
>
> The effect was as dramatic as any of the famous
> fountains of Europe....I am tremendously impressed with
> every detail of the park. It has set a new standard of beauty
> for this city and, in many respects for the world.[8]

Griswold also wrote to Mitchell & Ritchey, "Mellon Square park is a real
masterpiece of design. All the details show the tremendous amount of
careful thought you gave them. They are most intriguing and highly sat-
isfactory."[9] Interestingly, there is no record of such a letter to Simonds &
Simonds.

Where Credit is Due

In December 1953 Griswold fell out with John O. Simonds over a promotional piece in the *Pittsburgh Press* attributing the landscape plans for Mellon Square to Griswold and Associates.[10] While the firm paid for the advertisement and supplied materials, Griswold did not know that Mellon Square would be pictured or credited, "and was terribly disturbed and called us for a correction," according to a letter of apology from the *Press* to Simonds.[11] Griswold called Simonds the next day and wrote a letter expressing deep regret for "the damage it has done to our personal and professional relationship," adding:

> This incident is doubly regrettable because it has caused dissention within the very small ranks of our struggling profession. For years I have worked to build up our professional standing in the Community and it hurts very deeply to have you jump to the conclusion that I have intentionally or unintentionally done anything to take credit for anything you have done. The record will ultimately prove that this unfortunate incident has been no deviation from my personal regard for you or my devotion to the good of our profession.[12]

The newspaper did publish a correction, but the rift between these two significant landscape architects never completely closed.[13] Still, they continued to admire each other's work and just three years later, in 1958, their firms began a successful collaboration with each other, and with Ezra C. Stiles, on the first master plan for Allegheny County's Regional Parks.[14]

Mellon Square was a marked achievement. In the ensuing years, the project was widely credited with initiating the renewal of downtown Pittsburgh. In September 1956 the ACCD released *Pittsburgh and Allegheny County: An Era of Progress and Accomplishment*, which highlighted redevelopment projects undertaken to date, including Mellon Square.[15] In 1961 Mellon Square was featured on a giant post-card, showing a bird's-eye view of the corner of Smithfield Street and Oliver Avenue, overlooking the cascading fountain. [FIG. 75]

Greater Pittsburgh magazine later affirmed that Mellon Square sparked rebirth in the Golden Triangle, "culminating in towering new buildings fashioned from the products that are a major foundation of Pittsburgh's economy."[16] [FIG. 76]

The urban critic Jane Jacobs, in *Fortune's* historic 1958 issue "The Exploding Metropolis," saluted the role of urban fountains and the need for a project to add to a city's individuality:

> The use of color offers another way of building more liveliness into fountains. The cascade of Mellon Square in Pittsburgh offers a prime example. The cascade—great sheets of water pouring over a series of six graceful shelves alongside the stairway down to the Smithfield Street level—provides by day a shaded, water-splashed bit of landscape; by night, lit with colored lights, an exciting display.... Pittsburgh is on the right track at Mellon Square (an ideally located focal point), where the sidewalk gives way to tall stairways, animated by a

FIG. 76
The U.S. Steel/Mellon Bank
Building, by Harrison & Abramovitz
with Mitchell & Ritchey, featured
chevron-patterned aluminum
panels set between limestone
ribbon piers.

FIG. 77
Shopping expeditions to downtown
Pittsburgh usually included a visit
to Mellon Square.

cascade. This is a fine dramatization of
Pittsburgh's hilliness, and it is used nat-
urally where the street slopes steeply.[17]

Upon its completion, Mellon Square drew daily crowds of office
workers, shoppers, and other visitors to enjoy its geometric tranquility.
As the Mellons expected, city leaders worked to ensure that the plaza's
use was consistent with donor intentions and the City of Pittsburgh's
interests. The city established an advisory committee on Mellon Square,
composed of representatives from the Mayor's Office, the Department
of Parks and Recreation, the Law Department, City Council, and the
ACCD. In February 1956 the advisory committee released a policy statement that forbade a number of uses, including organized gatherings or
groups; commercial or industrial programs; signs, billboards, exhibits,
posters, or advertising; direct radio or television broadcasting from the
park without specific authorization; solicitation for charities in the park
or the immediate surrounding sidewalks; or any type of meeting, rally,
or program not specifically mentioned above except the city's official
Christmas presentation.[18] [FIG. 77]

The Necessity of Renewal

During its early years of operation, Mellon Square was continually fine-tuned to correct design and construction failures. Beginning in the winter of 1955–56, the ceramic tile in the main fountain area began to chip and spall in several areas. In 1956 an analysis by the Tile Institute determined it to be "soft tile," but the Mosaic Tile Company requested that the main fountain tile be allowed to weather through another winter so that more definite conclusions could be formed. From 1956 to 1957 the tile continued to disintegrate at an increased rate throughout the entire fountain area and the ACCD formally demanded the replacement of all tile "with new tile of good quality." They decided to install a nonglazed tile, and Ritchey agreed to prepare the shop drawings for the tile layout for no fee. In May 1958 full agreement was reached with respect to the tile pattern and colors in the main pool. Samples provided by the Mosaic Tile Company were tested for absorption, staining, and free-thaw patterns, and the unglazed tile was found to be acceptable. Subcontractor Rampa Marble & Tile Company began removing the deteriorated tile on May 7 and installed the new tile thereafter. The project was complete by July 4, 1958.

The city faced a number of additional obstacles at the plaza in the late-1950s. The location proved to be one of Pittsburgh's windiest streets, and prevailing west winds broke the quarter-inch galvanized steel guy-wires for 28 larger trees. In late October 1955 Eisler Nurseries was contacted to install 116 wrought iron rods with a ring on one end and a hook on the other end to replace the wires. During the winter of 1955 two small plantings of ivy and euonymus, situated on either side of one of the main entrances to the garage, died from constant exposure to warm air from adjacent exhaust ducts. The plants were replaced with block stone paving.

In October 1956 Park H. Martin wrote to the H. K. Ferguson Company regarding six items that appeared defective in the materials and workmanship: deterioration of ceramic tile; movement of granite wall and coping; drainage at base of steps on Smithfield Street; snow-melting apparatus; cam timer; and water dripping from the cascades. The hydraulics in the park posed additional problems. Department of Parks and Recreation laborers were unable to keep the fountains clean and presentable for more than two days in a row without draining, scrubbing, and refilling, and steps were taken to filter and soften the water in both pools.

The Department of Parks and Recreation investigated the condition of the plant material in early 1959, finding that severe winter weather had killed a large number of plants and weakened an additional quantity to such an extent that recuperation in the spring would be doubtful. Among the dead was ten thousand English ivy.

The large planting bed, also the shallowest, was completely devoid of plants, and other areas were also nearly empty. Later that year, Parks Director Robert J. Templeton wrote, "We believe this situation to be a serious emergency in as much as Mellon Square is the planting show place of the city and must be maintained properly at all times if the city is to escape undesirable public criticism."[19] Many of the plantings that did not survive were replaced, including linden trees damaged by warm air from adjacent large ventilator ducts. Five Waterer pines died within five years of planting and were replaced with large sheared upright Japanese yew. It was reported that the average cost of planting material for the plaza was $1,437.67 per year between 1956 and 1961.

By the mid-1960s public interest began to wane. In 1964 the Department of Public Works discussed a proposal to revise and vary the Christmas display at the park to arouse public attention and to use the park's facilities and setting to its best advantage.

As a result of disappointing experiences with the flowerbeds in 1964 and 1965, the City of Pittsburgh agreed that they should be eliminated (though, in fact, they were replanted as part of a downtown promotion scheme). Diminished maintenance also contributed to incremental deterioration. Yet despite declining enthusiasm for the plaza, it continued to be widely used and enjoyed, particularly for casual workday lunches in good weather.

Several years of trial and error followed, as the city experimented with different varieties and combinations of plants to suit the plaza's exposure to sun and the elements, as well as shallow planting areas. However, the forest composition of flowering and evergreen trees underplanted with ivy next to the main fountain was not replanted. The area was instead retained as a lawn panel and in 1977 received a stainless steel sculpture, *Forest Devil* by Kenneth Snelson, on loan from the Carnegie Museum of Art as part of the Three Rivers Arts Festival's Sculpturescape project.[20]

Though Mellon Square was no longer a maintenance priority, the city did take steps to sustain it. In June 1978 one hundred coleus and thirty-five begonia plants were replaced near the cascade fountain. The series of shallow planters next to the waterfall were constantly water-logged. City horticulturalist Ed Vasilcik suggested reconstructing this area to include deeper planting beds and to deflect the waterfall spray from the plantings.[21] Although no changes were made to the planters, deflectors were added to the cascade.

A Second Renaissance—The 1980s City Reimagined

The success of the city's renewal in the 1950s and '60s was the product of a new type of partnership that combined public authority with civic leadership and private funding. But in 1969 Mayor Peter Flaherty discontinued the public-private partnership that characterized the Pittsburgh Renaissance and instead advocated neighborhood renewal and tax reduction. Nonetheless, economic decline prevailed through the following decade. When Richard Caliguiri became mayor in 1976, the steel industry, once the powerhouse that drove the Pittsburgh region, was in sharp decline. In just four years, from 1980–84, the number of Pittsburghers working in the steel industry was cut by half. In 1980 just one-quarter's loss for U.S. Steel totaled $561 million. And the population of the city plummeted to 423,000 from a high of 676,000 in 1950. Unemployment rates skyrocketed. City leaders strove to reposition the local economy, based on high technology, health, education, riverfront development, and tourism.[22]

When Mayor Caliguiri renewed the public-private partnership that allowed development funding through the public authority in 1980, Renaissance II emerged with vigor to encourage corporate growth and the viability of downtown. Under the slogan "Jobs & Housing," the down-town development strategy included policies governing preservation, land use, and the relationship of new development to existing transportation systems; transportation improvements; strategies promoting and coordinating public open spaces; standards for street lighting, traffic controls, signage and street furniture; zoning and development controls; and priorities for using public investment to further overall development objectives.

Despite fluctuations in the economy, Renaissance II forged ahead through the 1980s, giving the city many of its signature skyline buildings, such as Mellon Bank Center, One Oxford Center, PPG Plaza, and Fifth Avenue Place. But its focus was on cultural and neighborhood development, not the remaking of city fabric as in its first Renaissance.

Rescuing the Plaza from Wear and Tear

By the early 1980s Mellon Square had experienced more than two decades of growth and use. "Physically, the facility is beginning to show its age," wrote Louise R. Brown, director of the Department of Parks and Recreation. "Building systems, pools, planting, waterproofing, finishes, etc., should be examined before serious problems occur."[23]

In 1981 the city asked EP&D to analyze the functional and physical needs of Mellon Square and to make recommendations. Priorities for improvements included electrical distribution, waterproofing, granite repair, terrazzo repair, and surface drainage repairs. When Brown appealed to the Richard King Mellon Foundation to fund the study, its trustees approved a grant of forty thousand dollars to the ACCD to commission a restoration plan. The study was intended to establish a "program, priorities, and funding to prepare this 'city treasure' for its next quarter century."[24]

For the study EP&D reviewed a variety of historical documents relating to the construction of Mellon Square and conferred with Simonds, then retired. Interviews were conducted with the ACCD, Department of Parks and Recreation, the Department of City Planning, adjacent building and property owners, and city-planning consultant Jonathan Barnett to gather information relating to issues regarding the Square.

The 1983 report, *Mellon Square Improvements*, opened with the statement that Mellon Square "is still one of the finest urban parks in our country," and included a historical chronology, a discussion of financing, and a recap of the donors' intention for a quiet haven of beauty, rest, and relaxation.[25] Three levels of recommendations were presented:

restoration and maintenance; appurtenances and facilities; and major elements and alternatives. According to Bob Vukich, who worked on the project at EP&D, "If [Simonds] had any involvement, it was slight."[26] While Simonds agreed with the need for updates, he was not happy with design changes to the fountains, according to Marjorie Simonds.[27]

The plaza was to be completely rewired and additional water-proofing given to the planting beds to prevent further leakage into the parking garage below. All granite components, damaged by vandalism and poor maintenance, were to be cleaned, repointed, and caulked, and replaced where needed. Surface drainage needed repair. Found to be in relatively good shape, the rustic terrazzo paving was to be repaired, cleaned, and resealed where needed. The report found that the overly mature and unhealthy plantings needed to be completely replaced, and recommended that the planting scheme be significantly modified.

The study recommended installing midstep handrails for stairs along Smithfield Street, and bollards at the William Penn Place entrances to prevent unauthorized vehicular use. Additional trash receptacles "compatible with the visual quality of the environment" were needed to handle excess trash from lunchtime users.[28]

Systems for the fountains needed to be restored to proper working order, but a major recommendation and a high priority of the client was to provide more places for people to sit. The only opportunity to do so was at the edge of the main fountain. The end result was a redesign of the main fountain with the added benefit of enhancing the "water to people contact." The water display itself was simplified by the removal of the grid of small water jets. Lighting was found to require major upgrades. The study recommended fully restoring the original lighting system, but acknowledged, "There is concern that this approach would not provide sufficient illumination and would be maintenance intensive because of the large number of fixtures." It added that "the historical character, however, would be preserved." A second option would have installed a rectangular pattern of pedestrian scale post light fixtures, but observed that it "would be a new and possibly disturbing element in the park."[29] Other options would have placed tall floodlights at the park's four corners or on the roofs of adjacent buildings. Two lines of flagpoles were proposed to exhibit banners designed by Pittsburgh artists; they had been in the original design and construction drawings but were never installed.

Sidewalks around Mellon Square were also studied. Two new sidewalks were to be constructed along Sixth Avenue and Oliver Avenue, and the existing sidewalks along Smithfield Street and William Penn Way rebuilt, all conforming to city standards for downtown—granite curb, granite strip for utility access, and rustic terrazzo paving.

EP&D also outlined priorities for projects requiring the most immediate attention. In order, priorities included electrical distribution, waterproofing, granite repair, terrazzo repair, surface drainage repairs, and lighting.

The possibility of improvements at Mellon Square provoked strong reactions from interested parties. After viewing a draft of the EP&D report, a city planning official responded, "Alterations should be minimal and should not seek to change the appeal of the park by adopting the latest fads....We have many opportunities for 1980s designs in 1980s projects."[30] The official rejected a proposed arbor as an "unnecessary addition" and an "unwise use of funds" as the park "does not require design changes to acquire users."[31]

Likewise, Barnett expressed his preference for a conservative approach for Mellon Square. He saw the original design as having been informed by a single sensibility, which could not be duplicated. "It's a period piece," he wrote, "and that period is over."[32] However, he was confident that the fountain could "be redesigned without doing violence to the overall integrity of the park."[33] Barnett disagreed with EP&D's Paul Wolfe, whom Barnett saw as promoting too many changes to the historic design. As a result, nothing was done.

Mid- to Late-1980s Work

During the mid-eighties, the condition of Mellon Square continued to decline. Water from the surface areas of the landscape leaked into the retail spaces along Smithfield Street and the parking garage below. The original five-ply tarpaper for waterproofing had not withstood thirty years of constant moisture. Deteriorated wiring caused several electrical fires. The main fountain and lighting no longer worked, and vegetation was in decline, the azalea and rhododendron understory completely absent.

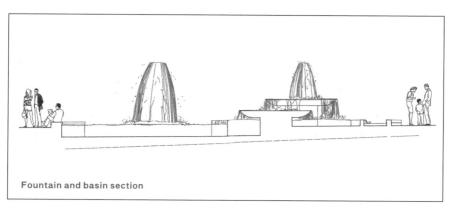

Fountain and basin section

Though the Mellons intended the plaza to be a quiet, contemplative space, by the 1980s the city wanted more public interaction within the park. Concerts were regularly held, requiring electrical capacity an seating areas for listeners. On many occasions, performers were located south of the main pool between planting beds, while the audience sat on nearby planter edges, fountain edges, and available benches. [**FIGS. 78 AND 79**] Throughout the 1980s Mellon Square became more regularly programmed for events, but it was on a make-do basis, without the capacity and infrastructure needed for this type of programmed use.

Community leaders finally rallied together to make improvements as outlined in EP&D's 1983 report. The city, ACCD, and PPA, among others, contributed funds to restore the thirty-year-old plaza. The Richard King Mellon Foundation donated $1,200,000 conditioned upon Mayor Caliguiri's guarantee that the city would improve and increase maintenance. The City of Pittsburgh requested a proposal for Mellon

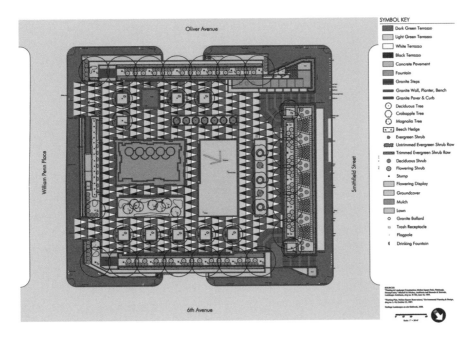

Oliver Avenue

William Penn Place

Smithfield Street

6th Avenue

SYMBOL KEY
- Dark Green Terrazzo
- Light Green Terrazzo
- White Terrazzo
- Black Terrazzo
- Concrete Pavement
- Fountain
- Granite Steps
- Granite Wall, Planter, Bench
- Granite Paver & Curb
- Deciduous Tree
- Crabapple Tree
- Magnolia Tree
- Beech Hedge
- Evergreen Shrub
- Untrimmed Evergreen Shrub Row
- Trimmed Evergreen Shrub Row
- Deciduous Shrub
- Flowering Shrub
- Stump
- Flowering Display
- Groundcover
- Mulch
- Lawn
- Granite Bollard
- Trash Receptacle
- Flagpole
- Drinking Fountain

FIG. 80
The late-1980s renovation plan emphasized programming, including concerts, replacing one tree planter with a stage, and retaining the Kenneth Snelson sculpture.

Square from EP&D for "a full range of services from evaluation of existing conditions through construction and as-built drawings."[34] EP&D published specifications on October 23, 1987, estimating the cost to be total of $3,126,680. [FIG. 80]

Available funding enabled Mellon Square to be rebuilt with certain changes. Construction began in April 1988. To facilitate the much-needed waterproofing and electrical system improvements, all granite pieces of the structure were numbered and catalogued for removal and storage during construction. The bronze fountain basins were removed and sent to the original foundry, Matthews International Corporation, the original foundry, for polishing and refinishing. The remainder of the plaza was dismantled to allow for the installation of new waterproofing, electrical wiring, and added power supply. A thin layer of SikaTop 111, a lightweight concrete, was poured on top of the structural slab of the parking garage to raise the plaza's surface to the necessary grade.

FIG. 81
Freshly renovated in 1990, Mellon
Square sustained four significant
alterations to its original form: the
main and cascade fountains, the
stage, and the sculpture lawn.

During construction, structural concerns arose regarding the condition of the concrete walls behind the granite panels of the planter walls and at the park entrance stairs. Areas of the exterior planter walls were found to have cracked and spalled, with some of the steel reinforcements exposed and oxidizing. The interior walls had evidence of delaminated waterproofing parging. The steps were also cracked and spalled, particularly in the areas of the corroded snow-melting system, which had broken the structural concrete. To repair the structural concrete, recommendations were made to remove and repair the waterproofing membrane in the planter areas and to remove the steam snow-melting system under the steps. A change order was issued to address the problems, and damaged elements were corrected.

With infrastructural improvements in place, the catalogued granite pieces were reinstalled in their original locations. More durable trench drains were placed to capture drainage throughout the plaza, and the triangular terrazzo paving was recreated by William Patrizio of Patrizio Art Mosaic Company, who did the original paving in the 1950s. The original light fixtures mounted within the planter walls were removed. As Bob Vukich recalled, "Our client didn't want to retain the lights. I thought that mounting stainless steel plates over the light openings was the best thing we could do. It was a durable material that would be easiest to deal with, while remaining in place as a signal to the future that the lights were missing and should be restored."[35] [FIG. 81] In an effort to increase park safety, floodlights were installed on the William Penn Hotel and the Oliver Building for a moonlight effect and additional light fixtures were placed along the newly constructed sidewalks surrounding the plaza. Handrails were added to the Smithfield Street steps, bollards were placed along the William Penn Place entrances, and additional trash receptacles were positioned throughout.

The work that occurred from 1987–89 made substantial changes to the original design. [FIG. 82] To increase capacity for concerts and other programs, one tree planter was replaced by a small, tiered stage platform. The main fountain was redesigned with granite seat walls. The cascade fountain was similarly modified with granite baffles placed at the edges to narrow the cascade, reduce turbulence, and prevent the water splashing onto the steps and planting beds. When rebuilt, the interior surfaces of the originally tiled fountains were changed to terrazzo to complement their new granite walls, which matched the planting beds.

The Snelson sculpture—though it was not original to the Simonds & Simonds design, nor site-specific or site-generated—was reinstalled. With the exception of the large rectangular bed containing the sculpture, the original planting design was respected with few significant changes. Good performers, such as sweetbay magnolia and little-leaf linden, were installed again, while substitutes were chosen for those plants that had difficulty growing in the urban environment. Overall, the original planting design intent was adhered to. Irrigation was also added to all planting beds.

Despite the efforts made in the late 1980s to address issues at Mellon Square, continued maintenance did not remain a priority. The annual budget decreased steadily, contributing to the plaza's second period of decline.

FIG. 82
Mellon Square continued to be
popular with Pittsburghers in 1995.

Partnering in Planning and Funding

Mellon Square remained an active place into the twenty-first century, but by 2007 it was, yet again, showing alarming signs of physical wear and tear. Its deterioration made the space feel rundown rather than vibrant—an impression that worked directly against the site's cultural and economic value, and which may have contributed to a high vacancy rate in adjacent commercial space.

Vegetation had been simplified, with some areas of planter beds denuded of groundcover and dying trees. Rats had infested the beds, lured in part by the leftovers from lunchtime and pigeon feeding. Large flocks of pigeons swooping low over the plaza frightened visitors, who found it difficult to find a clean stretch of bench for sitting among all the pigeon droppings. [FIG. 83] Above the storefronts along Smithfield Street, the large planter bed was a haphazard remnant of shrubs and precast pavers, attracting overnight sleepers who would bathe in the fountains come morning.

FIG. 83
Pigeon feeding was unchecked, soiling benches, attracting rats, and frightening some park visitors.

All automated fountain systems had failed. There was no anemometer control to reduce overspray on windy days, and the fountains only ran during the hours of 7:30 a.m. to 2:30 p.m. because a Public Works employee had to be on-site to manually clean filters on an almost hourly basis. [FIG. 84] In addition to the 1980s redesign of the fountains based on the same granite and terrazzo materials as in the original planters and paving, the form of the fountains also relied on the same geometries, but in stark contrast to the original fountain designs. The original main fountain, with its low convex edge and pastel surface, had provided a lighter, brighter, and more graceful character, which was shared by the cascade fountain—offering a delicate counterpoint to the granite planter boxes. After 1989 the heavy, baffled walls of the cascade and notched form of the central fountain no longer offered the contrast that was so essential to creating the light and refreshing quality of an oasis.

FIG. 84
By 2010 fountains were dry unless manually operated, plantings were overgrown or dead, and large portions of the perimeter terrazzo sidewalk had been replaced with standard broom-finish concrete.

FIG. 85
Fertilizer minerals leached onto the granite steps due to failed drainage systems and created a stone-like build-up.

FIG. 86
Clogged and cracked trench drains and deteriorated terrazzo allowed water movement through the pavement's gravel underlayer, leaking into the garage below.

FIG. 87
Alterations to the storefronts had obscured the elegant character of Mellon Square's original design.

Obstacles to public use mounted. The stair treads began to settle, creating uneven and dangerous height differentials. Mineral deposits from fertilizer built up a concrete-like layer on areas of the steps. [FIG. 85] Railings were loose. Drains were plugged. [FIG. 86] The terrazzo was dirty and breaking up in areas due to lack of routine cleaning and sealing, and the application of harsh salts during the winter season. Grease marks and chips from skateboarding and biking marred the granite edges. Storefront tenants under the overhanging canopy complained regularly of leaks from the planter above and the dark, dreary conditions. [FIG. 87] All of these obstacles combined to provide a prime opportunity to revisit the restoration of Mellon Square, and in the coming decades, several parties joined together to gain a newly revived public space in downtown Pittsburgh.

6

The Future of Mellon Square

To put a stop to the decay of this modern icon, the Pittsburgh Downtown Partnership in 2007 looked to the Pittsburgh Parks Conservancy, the city's private nonprofit partner in restoring and managing public parks. The organization's mission is to improve quality of life for the people of Pittsburgh by restoring the park system to excellence in partnership with government and community organizations. Founded in 1996, the Conservancy coproduced a master plan for the system of historic regional parks with the city, has completed numerous large capital projects, operates several park properties, and provides ecological management and environmental education. An operating agreement with the city encourages the Conservancy to extend its services to any park as time and resources allow, and based on that agreement the stage was set for the Conservancy to embrace Mellon Square.

Through funding from the Richard King Mellon Foundation and the Bank of New York Mellon (BNY), the Conservancy began work on the *Mellon Square Preservation, Interpretation, and Management Plan* in 2008. It was intended to be a comprehensive tool with which to undertake physical preservation, restoration, maintenance, and programming. The planning team was led by Patricia M. O'Donnell, and included specialists in cultural landscapes, engineering, lighting, and interpretation.[1]

A treasure trove of historical documents and plans was collected and studied to develop an understanding of the original design intent for Mellon Square, its construction, and change over time. EP&D's archives provided the most significant resource, including the earliest conceptual sketches and complete construction documents from 1955 and 1987. Extensive resources were also found at the University of Pittsburgh, University of Florida, Carnegie Mellon University, Carnegie Library, and Heinz History Center. These documents, drawings, and

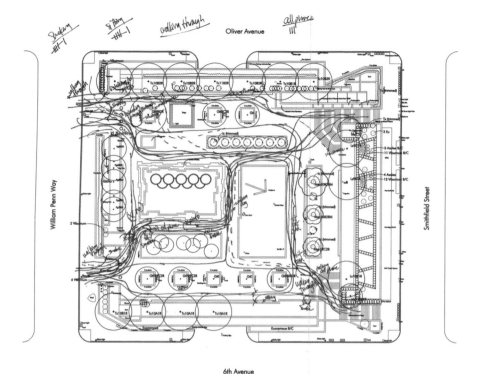

FIG. 88
As part of the 2009 planning effort,
pedestrian movements were
mapped to improve understanding
of activities and densities along
various corridors through the plaza.

photographs provided the basis for planning the project work and creating a rich interpretive program about shaping Pittsburgh through
Modernist landscape architecture.

Completed in 2009, the two-year planning effort aimed to recapture the strength of the original design, while attending to contemporary needs, public safety, and resource limitations. The plan promoted
enhanced sustainability and provided a rich interpretive agenda for the
Mellon Square landscape. Most importantly, the plan concluded that
the site's historical significance qualifies it for an individual listing in the
National Register of Historic Places, and possibly as a National Historic
Landmark.[2] Mellon Square meets three of the four eligibility criteria required for listing in the National Register of Historic Places, which is
maintained by the National Park Service.[3] The landscape, as O'Donnell
stated, "serves as a record of important historical movements, persons,
and artistic achievements in the mid-twentieth century."[4]

From a historic preservation perspective, Mellon Square has retained a high degree of integrity because its character and details today are recognizably the same as during its period of significance, the 1940s through 1980s. The spatial relationships, views, and pedestrian circulation had been maintained across time, along with the overall design effect of planting and water features. [FIG. 88]

Ways to Treat the Landscape

Many Modernist landscapes have met the wrecking ball over time. Even in its diminished state, Mellon Square was still loved by Pittsburghers and admired by design professionals. In preserving and restoring this work, it was important to recognize both its local value to everyday life, and its potential as a model for the national movement to preserve modern landscapes.

Preservation treatment is rooted in understanding the significance and integrity of a landscape.[5] The 2009 plan carefully considered Mellon Square's origins, evolution, and present condition to address its future direction. This approach was intended to yield a beautiful and accessible public landscape that preserved its seminal character-defining features while also addressing sustainability. A full understanding of contemporary needs, public safety, and resource limitations helped to shape a realistic plan that relied on the four types of preservation treatment, according to the Federal standards for historic landscape preservation.

Restoration is "the act or process of accurately depicting the form, features, and character of a property as it appeared at a particular period of time, by means of the removal of features from other periods in its history and reconstruction of missing features from the restoration period."[6] In the case of Mellon Square, historic documentation and resources were more than adequate to restore and recapture the original character, materials, and details. It was especially important to re-create the fountains and lush vegetation that defined the character of the original design.

Preservation is "the act or process of applying measures necessary to sustain the existing form, integrity, and materials of an historic property."[7] Preservation treatment for Mellon Square addressed the

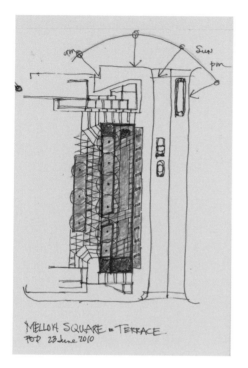

MELLON SQUARE - TERRACE
POP 23 June 2010

FIG. 89
An early study for the new terrace
explored a continuation of the
paving diagonal.

ongoing maintenance and repair of historic materials and features, such
as replacing broken granite slabs and deteriorating pavement.

Rehabilitation is "the act or process of making possible a compatible use for a property through repair, alteration, and additions while
preserving those portions or features that convey its historical, cultural,
or architectural values."[8] At Mellon Square the rehabilitation approach
was applied to the limited area above the retail spaces along Smithfield
Street, where the goals were to remove unkempt plantings, resolve
drainage problems, and increase and enhance useable public space.
It was crucial that the new terrace be compatible and carefully detailed
to integrate with the original design of the rooftop plaza, and yet be a
distinguishably contemporary alteration. [FIG. 89]

Throughout Mellon Square, the planting palette was evalu-
ated and rehabilitated. The original plant list was taken as the starting
point, and alternates were selected for better cold-hardiness or to re-
sist pest and disease conditions that would limit viability. For example,

spirea (*Spirea* spp.), hardy to Pittsburgh's Zone 4, replaced the more tender Zone 6 Japanese andromeda (*Pieris japonica*). A variety of native groundcovers on the plant list, such as bearberry (*Arctostaphylos uva-ursi*), were specified to reduce the reliance on ivies, of which only Baltic ivy remains. Because pigeons were observed to roost in the open canopies of the littleleaf linden trees, Persian ironwood (*Parrotia persica*) was chosen as the replacement in hopes that the larger leaves and denser canopy would be less inviting. For the very shallow planter, three types of pines were selected that typically grow in windy conditions on rocky, shallow soils at high elevations (see Appendix: Plant Lists, p. 152, for a comparison of the three periods of work).

Reconstruction is "the act or process of depicting, by means of new construction, the form, features, and detailing of a non-surviving site, landscape building, structure, or object for the purpose of replicating its appearance at a specific period of time and in its historic location."[9] In the case of Mellon Square, reconstruction was appropriate for the main fountain and cascade fountain. Their forms, water choreography, and lighting were to be reconstructed using a combination of precast and poured-in-place concrete, finished in a light celadon green color rather than tiled, in order to be durable and affordable.

Telling the Story

An important component of reviving Mellon Square was finding ways to effectively express the character and details of this significant cultural landscape to visitors. While people today are interested in using the plaza to escape the workplace, the number of users had dropped off significantly over the decades. A more engaging experience would attract more park users, who could behave as stewards of the park, supporting its ongoing maintenance and management goals.

Popular appreciation of Mellon Square will grow as the story is told in a variety of ways. Among the evolving concepts of historic conservation and preservation, the term *interpretation* no longer refers exclusively to public presentation—the familiar and carefully arranged display of historical facts and images to visitors through informational panels, walking tours, and other programs and media. The term also encompasses the public discussion of, and reflection upon, the role and

FIG. 90
Mellon Square richly
expresses "intangible
heritage," including the
"office lunch break,"
shown in 2009.

FIG. 91
A permanent interpretive display, located adjacent to the
storefronts, was designed to serve as an invitation to explore the
plaza above, to introduce the public to the story of Pittsburgh's
Renaissance and Mellon Square, and to give a visual lift to the
dark storefront facade. Individual panels were sized to replicate
the original windows and granite base.

significance of a particular cultural landscape, monument, or place in
the life of a contemporary community. Interpretation can also be considered as a tool for education, fundraising, lobbying, and management,
both on-site and off. Interpretive specialist Neil Silberman joined the
Mellon Square team to develop an interpretive program for the telling of
the plaza's value and history.[10] [FIG. 90]

One goal of the interpretive program is to provide a richer experience of Mellon Square's design and history in order to foster visitor
engagement. In response to this need, an interpretive wall introduces
visitors to the story of Mellon Square. [FIG. 91] Visually, its location adjacent to storefronts along Smithfield Street helps to reinstate the rhythm
and proportions of the storefront window design, and avoids intruding
on the core plaza space. The panels present a sidewalk gallery of striking images and brief text that summarizes key points in the storyline of
Mellon Square.

Other interpretive approaches can be taken over time to enhance public support and understanding. Future options may include
guided tours, educational workbooks and programs, as well as digital

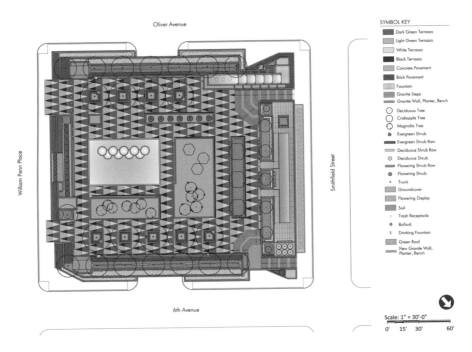

Oliver Avenue

William Penn Place

Smithfield Street

6th Avenue

SYMBOL KEY

Dark Green Terrazzo
Light Green Terrazzo
White Terrazzo
Black Terrazzo
Concrete Pavement
Brick Pavement
Fountain
Granite Steps
Granite Wall, Planter, Bench
Deciduous Tree
Crabapple Tree
Magnolia Tree
Evergreen Shrub
Evergreen Shrub Row
Deciduous Shrub Row
Deciduous Shrub
Flowering Shrub Row
Flowering Shrub
Trunk
Groundcover
Flowering Display
Soil
Trash Receptacle
Bollard
Drinking Fountain
Green Roof
New Granite Wall, Planter, Bench

Scale: 1" = 30'-0"

0'   15'   30'   60'

FIG. 92
Landscape Treatment Plan, 2011.

elements such as downloadable MP3 tours,
archival materials, and virtual tours.

Overall, the primary goal of interpretation in Mellon Square is not limited to providing the general public with historical information and design insights. It is to cultivate appreciation and support by a wide range of stakeholders in the ongoing efforts to present, maintain, and conserve this unique legacy of design as a public treasure.

A Sustainable Renewal

When the Conservancy set out to revive Mellon Square, it was on the basis of a well-researched and thoughtfully considered plan. But success also required strategic efforts. These included public outreach to encourage recognition of the plaza's value and change negative perceptions; effective fundraising to secure commitments to maintenance as well as restoration; reaching accord with the city as property owner and the PPA as principal tenant; as well as a strong commitment to quality through well-supported design decisions and pragmatic construction management.

FIG. 93
In 2009 the Cultural Landscape
Foundation, in collaboration
with the Pittsburgh Parks
Conservancy, presented a regional
symposium titled "The Hunter &
Philosopher: John O. Simonds
Pioneer Landscape Architect" at
Pittsburgh's Andy Warhol Museum.
At the podium, Robert Vukich
recalled working with Simonds.

FIG. 94
In 2011 the Conservancy
commissioned artist Bob Bowden
to create a watercolor painting of
Mellon Square as it would appear
upon completion.

The opening salvo in the campaign to save Mellon Square was a speech presented in early 2007 to civic leaders by Charles Birnbaum. Speaking from his perspective as president of The Cultural Landscape Foundation, and with a commitment to preserving modern landscape architecture, Birnbaum revealed the plaza's status as a work of design genius, declaring it "a nationally significant landscape."[11] This event gave tremendous credence and momentum to the idea of preserving and restoring, rather than redesigning, the ailing icon.

Within months the Richard King Mellon Foundation and BNY Mellon granted funding to the Conservancy to produce a plan for the revival of Mellon Square. Along with the funding came a clear mandate to find a sustainable solution to the longstanding maintenance challenge, since the Richard King Mellon Foundation had funded the 1987 work and did not want to contemplate yet another cycle of improvement and decline, with the inevitable future request for funding.

The planning team devoted the first half of 2008 to discussions with stakeholders, historic research, park use studies, lighting review, and analysis of all the findings. During the summer a structural engineering study was completed and themes for cultural interpretation were conceived. From this knowledge base, the team developed treatment concepts from late summer into early fall. [FIG. 92]

In keeping with Silberman's recommendations for the interpretive program, the Conservancy embarked on a series of public speaking engagements, which have continued since the project's conception. Audiences have included preservationists, tour guides, private developers, realtors, small business owners, downtown workers and residents, civic organizations, and design and planning professionals. [FIG. 93]

Pittsburgh Quarterly magazine and the *Pittsburgh Tribune-Review* both published in-depth articles on the project. The Conservancy commissioned celebrated watercolor artist Robert Bowden to create a painting to show how Mellon Square would look after completion, and an evening view to show lighting effects. [FIG. 94] These images were used on informational banners at the plaza, and in print materials for funding support. A graphic representation of the signature paving pattern became a recognizable icon of the project.

Upon completion of the preservation plan in 2009, the Conservancy introduced an audio tour for Mellon Square. Funded by the Benter Foundation, the tour consisted of narrated segments that could be accessed by telephone, as indicated by discreet signs placed around the plaza. Topics included Mellon Square's name, the pioneering concept of a park over a parking garage, the Pittsburgh Renaissance, the original design and changes over time, and Simonds.

Investment

As a direct result of these outreach efforts, interest and support began to mount. An important component of the case for restoration was the economic impact study commissioned by the Conservancy in 2010.[12] Produced by 4Ward Planning the study reinforced the lesson of 1955— that Mellon Square has a tremendous influence on surrounding property values and tax revenues. Moreover, its renovation and future mainte- nance would stimulate another surge in property values and boost rev- enues of nearby businesses.

Lead gifts for the renovation project and maintenance fund came from the Richard King Mellon Foundation, Colcom Foundation, and Eden Hall Foundation. The Conservancy then established the Committee for Mellon Square, with Mellon's sons Richard P. Mellon and Seward Prosser Mellon serving as honorary cochairs. It was a tremendously important endorsement for the project. [FIG. 95]

In light of the repeated failures by the city to consistently and adequately maintain Mellon Square, it was critically important for the Conservancy to define a long-term role for itself as operator and to establish the concept of a permanent maintenance fund. Staff mem- bers developed a pro forma annual budget, based on the Conservancy's track record of managing the five-acre Schenley Plaza in the Oakland section of Pittsburgh. The budget addressed routine and preventive maintenance, security, and program management. Based on that bud- get, a $4 million goal was set for the maintenance fund devoted to perpetual stewardship of Mellon Square.

FIG. 95
Seward Prosser Mellon, honorary cochair of the Committee for Mellon Square, at the formal groundbreaking ceremony in June 2011.

Equally vital was crafting an operating agreement between the city and the Conservancy. The agreement requires the city to continue providing its current level of maintenance resources, with the Conservancy meeting custodial, security, programming, and repair needs for the plaza. The renewable operating agreement has a twenty-nine-year term.

Throughout the project, the PPA has also been a key partner, from input on planning and design, to cost-sharing for a final structural engineering study prior to construction. Since the agency controls the leased retail premises as well as the garage, it has also helped with tenant communications, especially important in developing the concept for the Smithfield facade, and during construction, such as when the terrace leaked into their spaces below.

Design and Construction

To a great degree, the Conservancy's work has focused on returning Mellon Square to its original design intent.[13] One might expect that process to be fairly simple and straightforward, given the complete documentation of the original construction plans and specifications. However, the task was complicated due to the 1987–89 renovations, which had dismantled the plaza to update its waterproofing.

Some assumptions made during the design process proved to be false once construction was underway. For example, demolition of the central fountain revealed that original drainage pipes had been cut off but not removed during the eighties' work, which created passages for water to drain through the gravel layer under the pavement, infiltrating the garage. This explained the leaks and corrosion within the parking garage stair tower.

Drainage was, of course, a principal concern. Complaints of leakage into the garage and tenant spaces had to be addressed in the renovation. Green roof technology, such as waterproofing materials and drainage systems, had finally caught up with the innovative concept of Mellon Square as one of the first rooftop plazas, and so the project was a prime opportunity to update. When planter boxes were emptied of soil, it was clear that the waterproofing materials had failed. Wherever exposed, the 1989 waterproofing system was removed and a new layer of waterproofing was applied on top of the original 1955 membrane because it provided a clear boundary line between the city's responsibilities above and the PPA below. [FIG. 96] Where mineral deposits had marred the granite treads of the stairs, new trench drains were added to the system, the treads were removed, and the waterproofing system was applied throughout. [FIG. 97]

The planted rooftop above the retail spaces was most subject to leaks, and so was transformed into a new terrace. It was essential to make this a universally accessible space. Since the level of the plaza was much higher than the terrace floor, it had to be built up so that a ramp of less than 5 percent slope could be achieved. [FIG. 98] During the many options studied, the largest concern was the placement of entrances to the terrace through the existing linden tree planter.

Additional exploration determined that the structural slab would have to be penetrated if the ramps were to begin within the planter areas, so studies focused on bringing the entrances through the planters on grade to landings, and then using stairs and a ramp for the change of grade. Two entrances were placed toward the center of the planter so they wouldn't be immediately seen as people enter the plaza's two main corridors leading from William Penn Place toward Smithfield Street. Ultimately, the design team settled on a nearly symmetrical arrangement of twin passages and ramps to provide the most flexibility in circulation, a consistent and inclusive experience of the new space, and simplicity of form. [FIGS. 99]

Much thought was also given to material selection and details, with the goal of giving the terrace subtle distinction from the historic design of Mellon Square. For example, stainless steel skate deterrents were installed on new granite benches within the terrace; elsewhere, stone cleats were made to match the original granite benches, curbs, and planter walls. [FIG. 100] The same rustic terrazzo paving was used, but without a diagonal pattern and in a mix of black, gray, and white (the city's sidewalk standard), to complement the granite planter walls. It was also a departure in scale: the smaller dimension of 5 feet by 2.5 feet makes the grid pattern visually recognizable, yet decidedly different from the triangular/harlequin pattern of the overall plaza. [FIG. 101] Pfaffman and Associates designed the parapet safety barrier along

FIG. 96
When the first planter boxes were emptied to make way for the new terrace, the failure of waterproofing systems was evident. So, too, was the extent of grade change that would have to be overcome so that the terrace could be made accessible.

FIG. 97
Stair treads were reinstalled after new waterproofing material and additional trench drains were placed.

FIG. 98
Conservancy Project Manager Phil Gruszka checks levels prior to pouring lightweight concrete over the blueboard (rigid foam insulation), which was used to build up the terrace subsurface.

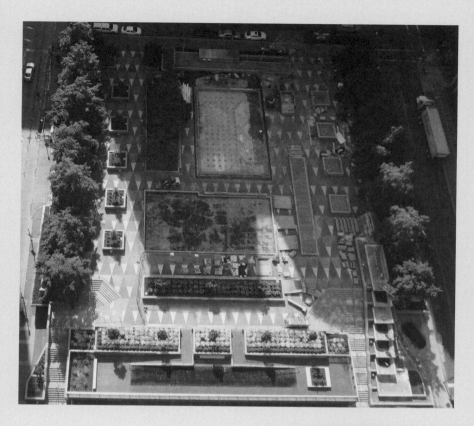

FIG. 99
As the first area to be completed, the terrace provides an exciting vantage point overlooking the restored cascade fountain and the activity of people moving along the main stairway.

FIG. 100
Skate deterrents were fabricated from "Iridian" granite, matching the original benches and curbs, for a more subtle appearance. To further differentiate new from historic, stainless steel cleats were applied to "Georgia Gray" granite used on the terrace.

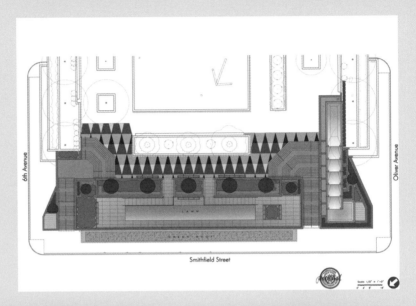

FIG. 101
Accessibility drove the final terrace
plan, with the paired entrances
located to avoid key sightlines from
within the plaza.

FIG. 102
Bordering the terrace, a
comfortably contoured aluminum
handrail conceals LED lighting
that subtly illuminates the woven
stainless steel mesh panels below.

FIG. 103
A carpet of mixed sedums
converted the storefront canopy
roof to a pleasant view from the
terrace and yet gives another
signal to the surrounding city that
a park lies just a flight up the stairs
from Smithfield Street.

the terrace perimeter with the goal of achieving transparency from the street-level view, to avoid the appearance of an additional wall above the storefronts. It is a stainless steel post and infill mesh system with a brushed satin finish. Extruded aluminum with a clear anodized finish is used for the upper horizontal rail to complement the stainless steel. Composed of individual stainless rods, the mesh infill panel has an over-all textured appearance that gives a shimmering quality to the space. The aerodynamically contoured handrail speaks to Mellon Square's modern heritage while concealing continuous LED lighting. [FIG.102] Just beyond and below the parapet barrier, the storefront canopy roof was laid with a carpet of mixed sedums to absorb rainwater and introduce a visible fringe of green from street level. [FIG.103]

Where new end walls had to be constructed for the two pas-sages cut through the historic linden tree planters to provide terrace ac-cess, the historic "Iridian" granite was matched. A different granite was selected for use elsewhere on the terrace to be distinguishable from, yet complementary to, the original. New benches, planter walls, curbs, and ramp walls are made of "Georgia Gray" granite, polished to match the historic stone finish. The profile and the finishes of the benches were completed in the manner of the existing ones in the plaza. [FIG.104]

The cascade fountain was reconstructed to match the char-acter and form of the original design, with curved basin edges that sur-round the five descending cascade pools as well as the upper and lower basins. Its concrete basins, including the upper and lower water reser-voirs, were cast in place, with only a slight variation to the coping height to better contain the water in windy conditions. A waterproof sealant was custom-tinted to achieve a grayish-green celadon color that would give an impression of lightness similar to the overall look of the original tiles. [FIG.105]

Of primary focus was the restoration of the main fountain. Relying on the 1954 construction drawings, the restoration design in-corporated the original cantilevered profile, the freeform curves of the large spray ring, and the gridded pattern of smaller fountain jets. All the original penetrations for plumbing and electrical service were located and reused. [FIGS.106] A combination of precast and poured-in-place concrete was employed to recreate the main fountain's pool-like shape.

FIG. 104
Finer-grained "Georgia Gray"
granite was selected for use on the
new terrace's benches, planters,
and curbs to complement, rather
than mimic, the plaza's original
Iridian granite.

FIG. 105
Reconstruction of the cascade
fountain required two weeks to
complete the first form due to its
very complex geometries.

FIG. 106
Restoring the waterworks called for
fabricating a new spray ring in the
original amoeba shape to reinstate
the most dramatic feature of the
main fountain.

TOP LEFT: FIG. 107
Workers use a custom-cut board to
screed the fountain into its subtle
concave form.

TOP RIGHT: FIG. 108
Precast concrete copings replicated
the original contour, while adding a
raised rib as a skate deterrent.

FIG. 109
After removing green paint, a
medium-brown bronze patina was
restored to the nine basins using
the classic hot wax method.

FIG. 110
The basins were reinstalled on new
columns after the main fountain was
waterproofed.

[FIGS. 107 AND 108] The bronze basins were removed by their original fabricator, now known as Matthews International, for restoration. Green paint was sandblasted from the surface, the battered drip edge replaced, and a patina applied in the classic hot wax process.[14] [FIG. 109] Close study of period photographs informed the choice of an overall medium brown patina mottled with burnished highlights and a golden patina on the curved lip of the basins. [FIG. 110]

Construction commenced in June 2011, with demolition and clearing of the area above the retail shops on Smithfield Street. The Conservancy acted as general contractor and began the project as a phased effort. Fundraising success ushered in an overlapping Phase II, which continued uninterrupted through the completion of the project in May 2014. As Meg Cheever stated,

> This park is a work of art that does not hang on the wall of a museum, it sits out here in the open and is free and open to all the people of our city, and as we work together, we are looking forward to restoring the park, reclaiming it and giving it back to the people of Pittsburgh in as good condition as possible.[15]

The revival of Mellon Square represents a remarkable partnership between the Conservancy, City of Pittsburgh, PPA, Pittsburgh Downtown Partnership, and Pittsburgh History & Landmarks Foundation. With the combined efforts of these partners, plus the philanthropic community, civic and business leaders, design professionals, and skilled contractors, today's Mellon Square is a refreshing haven for workers, visitors, and residents, while supporting economic growth in the heart of downtown.

Major steps are being taken toward fulfilling the vision of the economic impact study. Reinvestment in surrounding, largely vacant, properties has surged dramatically. PNC Bank purchased the former Mellon Bank Building and rehabilitated it as a service center with more than seven hundred employees in 2013, reopening long-closed windows overlooking the plaza. The former Saks Building is to be replaced by a parking garage over ground-floor retail, with a residential tower to

FIG. 111
The conceptual design for the Smithfield Street frontage features the Interpretive Wall and uniform treatment of windows, signage, and lighting.

come in a later phase. A condominium conversion is set for the upper floors of the Regional Enterprise Tower (formerly the Alcoa Building). Two new hotels will bring more visitors to Mellon Square. Kimpton Hotels & Restaurants is redeveloping the former James H. Reed building into a Hotel Monaco, planned to open in late 2014. The upper floors of the Henry W. Oliver Building are being converted into an Embassy Suites Hotel with a projected opening in 2015.

To continue boosting the contribution made by Mellon Square to the downtown's quality of life and economic development, the Conservancy produced a conceptual design for the storefronts and perimeter in early 2014. Pfaffman & Associates led the design effort, which incorporated and expanded upon the renovation plan's recommendations. These included restoring and updating the architectural aesthetic of the original storefronts, identifying opportunities for improving the retail mix, and improving pedestrian entrances to the parking garage. [FIG. 111]

The constituency for Mellon Square, and its base of popular support, is consistently being enlarged by the addition of neighboring workers, residents, business travelers, and tourists. Once again Mellon Square lives up to the judgment of noted architectural historian James van Trump, who in 1983 declared it "the most effective piece of site planning in Pittsburgh." He added that "this elegant outdoor living room has been very well tied in to the surrounding old downtown neighborhood...'geared' to the people who use it, and it is *used*, which is not the least test of the fitness of any urban space."[16]

On a clement afternoon in the plaza, hundreds of people walk through and relax to catch a bit of sunshine and fresh air. Tourists and business travelers appreciate the verdant and urbane space, which speaks well of the city's values. Workers pour out into the open space beneath nearby skyscrapers to escape their cubicles and computer monitors. Concerts and other programs attract a crowd, but most people still seek the place of rest and refreshment that Mellon envisioned half a century ago—an oasis in the midst of the city. [FIG. 113]

Mellon Square is an iconic Modernist landscape. It is one of America's great urban spaces that have stood the test of time. Well-studied in schools of landscape architecture and urban design, Mellon Square has inspired designers around the world. Its influence can be seen in such diverse settings as Denver's Harlequin Plaza and Dubai's Tower Plaza. And once again, Mellon Square is a symbol of Pittsburgh's astounding capacity for reinvention and self-improvement—of what a city can achieve when it decides to remake itself.

Inspired by memories of Pittsburgh's Renaissance I, when Mellon and Mayor Lawrence forged their historic partnership, a new community partnership came together to reclaim this rare Modernist masterpiece. The goal has been to erase the ravages of time and to return the legacy of a master designer of modern landscape to the people of Pittsburgh, to restore it to the place of beauty, rest, and relaxation envisioned by Mellon, and to recreate an oasis in the heart of the Renaissance city of Pittsburgh.

FIG. 112
Architectural illustrator Edward
F. Dumont, who worked at
Environmental Planning & Design
early in his career, created this
rendering in 2012 to depict Mellon
Square as it would appear when
completed.

Epilogue

John O. Simonds: Philosopher, Author, Educator

Barry W. Starke, FASLA

Getting to know John O. Simonds and helping to tell the story of this passionate, insightful, and self-effacing man have been among the most rewarding experiences of my career.

At age six John's father told him, "The important thing in life is that the world be a better place because you have traveled through it." Late in life John would say, "In trying, I have come to believe that no other profession affords a better opportunity than Landscape Architecture."[1]

With this moral compass and guiding philosophy, John became one of the most multifaceted, visionary landscape architects in the profession's history. In awarding him the one-time President's Centennial Medal in 1999 "for unsurpassed contributions to the profession of Landscape Architecture in the past one hundred years," the American Society of Landscape Architects said, "John Simonds has done it all—a leading private practitioner, renowned author, outstanding educator....His professional leadership...is unequaled among his peers."[2] As ASLA President at the time, it was an honor to personally present John with this medal.

As a child John loved the great outdoors and immersed himself in it. With an insatiable appetite for "finding things out," John learned ecology by observing nature—knowledge later reinforced as an undergraduate at Michigan State University.

In his third year John decided to take leave and expand his knowledge through travel. Alone, he boarded a tramp steamer headed for Asia—a bold step for a youth of twenty. In Japan, John studied its people and culture, expanding his thinking about man and nature. His next stop was Borneo where a job awaited him but never materialized. By quirk of fate, he was befriended by an

English-speaking native, who invited John to come live among his indigenous tribal people—cannibals and headhunters who had inspired adventure books from John's childhood. Living with these hunter-gatherers as part of the land profoundly influenced John's understanding of man and nature as one.

In 1936 John entered Harvard where his developing philosophy first began to express itself. Graduating as a member of the infamous 1939 "class of rebels," John was clearly one of its environmental voices and broadest thinkers. Following graduation, John traveled back to Asia to study Zen and Tao.

Upon returning to Pittsburgh to set up practice, the die had been cast; everything he did from then on reflected his deep-seated philosophy of man and nature as one—the inseparability of humans from their environment and earth as the "human habitat."

John went on to share the spotlight as one of the most prolific professional authors of his time, producing four influential books: *Landscape Architecture*, *Freeway in the City* (with others), *Garden Cities 21*, and *Earthscape*.[3] As a consultant on countless boards, commissions, and task forces, serving legislators, governors, and a U.S. president, John wrote hundreds of planning documents, most of which were cutting-edge works of their time.

When first published in 1961 *Landscape Architecture* had an immediate impact on the profession, helping usher in the environmental movement. John published second and third editions while he was still alive. By inviting me to coauthor the fourth and subsequent editions, he facilitated its future publication beyond his lifetime. John considered this book his most important professional achievement. Although John did not write *Landscape Architecture* as a textbook, it became the textbook of choice worldwide soon after it was first published.

With simple graphics and inspirational text, it explained the comprehensive practice of this complex profession. Professor Kay Williams, FASLA noted, "As a student in the 1970s, I devoured Simonds's book....It was contemporary, yet it was timeless in its processes and thoughtfulness and respect for the land and all who share it."[4] John, through this book alone, contributed to the education of thousands of landscape architects for over fifty years and will continue to do so into the indefinite future.

John was not a professional educator *per se*. His classroom teaching experience was from 1955 to 1967 as a part-time faculty member at what is now Carnegie Mellon University. However, everything he wrote, said, and did had an educational purpose. What most would consider his "teachings" were the several hundred lectures and speeches delivered throughout the world during his career.

John O. Simonds died in 2005 at age ninety-two. Upon his death his son Todd wrote, "He practiced and preached landscape architecture with religious fervor, because it was his religion. The quest for harmony between man and the natural world was Dad's vocation, his calling, and he answered that calling as passionately and as well as any man ever could."[5]

Barry W. Starke, FASLA, is president of Earth Design Associates Inc. in Casanova, Virginia; former President of the American Society of Landscape Architects; and coauthor of the fourth and fifth editions of Landscape Architecture.

Notes

Editor's Foreword:
Polishing the Jewel

1. The Cultural Landscape Foundation, in collaboration with The Pittsburgh Parks Conservancy, held the symposium, "The Hunter and the Philosopher: John O. Simonds Landscape Architect" at the Andy Warhol Museum, Pittsburgh, Pennsylvania, on November 5, 2009. To learn more go to: http://tclf.org/sites/default/files/microsites/pioneers/pittsburgh/index.html.

Preface:
Telling the Story of a Masterwork

1. Pittsburgh Parks Conservancy, *Mellon Square: Preservation, Interpretation & Management Plan* (Pittsburgh: Pittsburgh Parks Conservancy, 2009).
2. Ibid., I.1.

Prologue:
The Simonds Way

1. Charles Birnbaum, "Mellon Square: A Nationally Significant Public Space," (paper presented at the Pittsburgh Golf Club for the Pittsburgh Parks Conservancy, in association with the City of Pittsburgh, The Carnegie Museum of Art, Chatham College Landscape Programs, and the Pittsburgh Downtown Partnership, Pittsburgh, Pennsylvania, February 1, 2007).

Chapter 1:
Designing Experiences

1. James A. Mitchell and Dahlen K. Ritchey, *Pittsburgh in Progress* (Pittsburgh: Kaufmann's Department Store, 1947).
2. Jill E. Pearlman, *Inventing American Modernism: Joseph Hudnut, Walter Gropius, and the Bauhaus Legacy at Harvard* (Charlottesville: University of Virginia Press, 2007), 2.
3. Michael Baker Jr. "Civic Arena (Public Auditorium)," Historic American Buildings Survey Report, HABS No. PA-6780, (Washington, D.C.: U.S. Department of the Interior, National Park Service, 2011).
4. James A. Mitchell and Dahlen K. Ritchey, "Impressions and Reflections," *Charette* (Pittsburgh: Pittsburgh Architectural Club, July and August 1937), 17–7:1–2 and 17–8:1–2.
5. Martin Aurand, "Mitchell & Ritchey Collection," Carnegie Mellon University Architecture Archives, accessed January 9, 2014, http://www.andrew.cmu.edu/user/ma1f/ArchArch/mitchell&ritchey.html.
6. Edward Mitchell (son of James A. Mitchell), interview with the author, September 18, 2013.
7. John O. Simonds, *Landscape Architecture: A Manual of Site Planning and Design* (New York: McGraw-Hill, 1961).
8. Marjorie Simonds, interview with the author, October 2, 2009.
9. John O. Simonds to Stuart Dawson, September 11, 1991.
10. Pearlman, *Inventing American Modernism*, 4.
11. "Lester Collins," the Cultural Landscape Foundation, accessed January 2014, http://tclf.org/pioneer/lester-collins. Lester Collins had a bachelor of arts in English and returned to Harvard after his travels with Simonds to earn a landscape architecture degree from Harvard in 1942.
12. Marjorie Simonds, interview.
13. Ibid.
14. Ibid.
15. Ibid. Mrs. Simonds recalled his manner of devotion—in all things—to be uninterruptable. The couple had four children, Taye, John Todd, Polly, and Leslie, and seven grandchildren.
16. After privatization in 1991, the Aviary was given national status by the U.S. Congress in 1993 and renamed the "National Aviary in Pittsburgh." A subsequent capital campaign and renovation project modernized the facility.
17. "Allegheny Commons," National Register of Historic Places, Reference number 13000740, (Washington, D.C.: National Park Service, 2009), accessed December 15, 2013, http://www.nps.gov/history/nr/feature/places/pdfs/13000740.pdf. The Allegheny Commons master plan produced in 2001 by Pressley Associates concluded that Lake Elizabeth and its surrounding landscape features were significant and intact and should be preserved, rather than returning its form and character to the Victorian era.
18. Philip D. Simonds, "The Birth of a Regional Park System," *Landscape Architecture Quarterly* (April 1963): 207-208. In addition to Simonds & Simonds, the other two firms engaged to design and develop the county parks were Ezra C. Stiles and Griswold, Winters and Swain.

19. John O. Simonds, Vincent Lecture (presented at the University of Georgia, Athens, Georgia, April 2, 1985). Courtesy of Hargrett Rare Book and Manuscript Library / University of Georgia Libraries.

20. Ibid.

21. Simonds & Simonds expanded into community planning in the 1960s, particularly in southern Florida. Largely due to Simonds's long-time friend Lester Collins, who joined the firm in 1955 as a Washington, D.C.–based partner, the politically prominent Graham family invited the firm to develop a plan for one thousand acres of property that would become the new community of Miami Lakes. Simonds then made a strategic decision to open an office in Miami Lakes that would serve as a base from which to address the wasteland of Floridian development. Bob Graham went on to become the 38th Governor of Florida (1979–87) and a U.S. Senator (1987–2005). He was a lifelong advocate for landscape architecture and conservation, helping to pass one of the nation's earliest comprehensive landscape architecture practice acts, and championing the restoration of the Everglades. Throughout his career, Graham relied on his relationship with Lester Collins and John O. Simonds. As Graham wrote in the foreword to Simonds's *Garden Cities 21,* "I am proud to be a friend of John Simonds. Through his writings and work, he has done much to advance the cause of sensitive landscape planning and to show that people, their communities, and cities can be brought into more productive, compatible, and rewarding relationship with the Earth." Reflective of this scope, Simonds & Simonds changed its name to Environmental Planning & Design Partnership (EP&D) in 1970.

22. *Landscape Architecture* (New York: McGraw-Hill, 1961, 1993, 1997, and revised with Barry Starke in 2006, 2013); *Earthscape: A Manual of Environmental Planning* (New York: Van Nostrand Reinhold Company, 1978); *Garden Cities 21: Creating a Liveable Urban Environment* (New York: McGraw-Hill, 1994).

23. Simonds retired from EP&D in 1983, continuing as partner emeritus, and also consulting privately through 1997, notably on the Paris Pike Bluegrass project in Lexington, Kentucky. Throughout his career, Simonds was active in education and service, teaching in the department of architecture at Carnegie Mellon University from 1955 to 1967 and lecturing at other schools throughout the world. Simonds was president of the American Society of Landscape Architects (ASLA) from 1963–65 and chaired the White House Conference on Natural Beauty in 1965. He served on the Federal Highway Beautification Commission (1965–66); the Board of Urban Advisors, Federal Highway Administration (1966–68); the President's Task Force on Resources and the Environment (1968–70); and the Design Advisory Panel for "Operation Breakthrough," U.S. Department of Housing and Urban Development (1970–74).

24. John O. Simonds, "A Sense of Mission" (Commentary for inclusion in the 1999 Centennial History of Landscape Architecture, July 17, 1998, John O. Simonds Collection, Special and Area Studies Collections, George A. Smathers Libraries, University of Florida, Gainesville, Florida, 1998).

Chapter 2:
The Genesis of Mellon Square: Design for a New Era

1. "Plaza," The Cultural Landscape Foundation, accessed January 28, 2014, http://tclf.org/content/plaza. Mellon Square is appropriately referred to as a "plaza," because it is a paved public gathering space. "Plazas are spatial volumes as much as paved surfaces; they bring light and air into the city, contrasting with adjacent streets that are often shaded due to their narrower width. By the mid-twentieth century, designers adapted the plaza typology to new commuter required infrastructure, adapting them to such spaces as the roofs of below grade parking garages, and to urban sites that emerged out of the demolition of urban renewal. As with pedestrian malls, courtyards, atria, and roof gardens, the creation of plazas has extended the functional landscape into the built environment, significantly enriching the visitor experience."

2. Roy Lubove, *Twentieth-Century Pittsburgh: Government, Business, and Environmental Change* (New York: John Wiley & Sons, 1969), 126.

3. James A. Mitchell, Dahlen K. Ritchey, and George S. Richardson, *Parking Park Study: A City Park and Underground Parking Garage for Pittsburgh's Golden Triangle* (Pittsburgh: Regional Planning Authority, 1949).

4. "Hotel LaSalle Garage," accessed September 2013, http://www.landmarks.org/

chicago_watch_2004_3.htm and http://www.
encyclopedia.chicagohistory.org/pages/959.
html.

5. "Union Square Then and Now," Visit Union
    Square, accessed October 2013, http://www.
    visitunionsquaresf.com/about_union_square/
    then_and_now/.

6. Rand Richards, *Historic San Francisco: A
    Concise History and Guide* (San Francisco:
    Heritage House Publishers, 2007), 54.

7. Jon Lang, *Urban Design: A Typology of
    Procedures and Products* (Oxford: Elsevier,
    2005), 90–93. Pershing Square was com-
    pletely redesigned in 1994 by architect Ricardo
    Legorreta of Legorreta Arquitectos and land-
    scape architect Laurie Olin of Hanna/Olin.

8. "Pittsburgh Downtown Central Historic
    District," National Register of Historic Places,
    Reference Number 13000251 (Washington,
    D.C.: National Park Service, 2013), accessed
    January 2014, http://www.nps.gov/nr/feature/
    places/13000251.htm.

9. American Planning Association, "American
    Planners Recognize 30 Great Neighborhoods,
    Streets, and Public Spaces," news release,
    October 8, 2008, https://www.planning.org/
    newsreleases/2008/oct08.htm.

10. Pennsylvania Historical & Museum
    Commission, "Late Woodland Period in the
    Susquehanna and Delaware River Valleys,"
    accessed January 2014, http://www.portal.
    state.pa.us/portal/server.pt/community/
    native_american_archaeology/3316/late_wood-
    land_period/406837. This period was a time
    of social and economic change, in which the
    atlatl was replaced by bow and arrow, and
    most groups relied on a mixed food economy,
    settling into villages and eventually warring
    against each other.

11. Sarah Hutchins Killikelly, *The History of
    Pittsburgh: Its Rise and Progress* (Pittsburgh:
    B.C. & Gordon Montgomery Company, 1906),
    80.

12. "The History of Market Square," Market Square
    Merchants Association, accessed January
    2014, http://marketsquarepgh.com/history.
    html.

13. Franklin Toker, *Pittsburgh, An Urban Portrait*
    (University Park, PA: Pennsylvania State
    University Press, 1986), 13.

14. *Downtown: A Golden Triangle* (Pittsburgh:
    University of Pittsburgh Press, 2009), 41.
    See also "Walking Tours of the Golden
    Triangle," Local Answers, accessed

January 2014, http://local.answers.
com/g/pittsburgh/neighborhoods/
walking-tours-of-the-golden-triangle.

15. "Mellon Square," City of Pittsburgh, accessed
    August 2013, http://www.city.pittsburgh.pa.us/
    wt/html/mellon_square.html.

16. "American Sign Language: Pittsburgh,"
    Lifeprint, accessed October 2013, http://www.
    lifeprint.com/asl101/pages-signs/p/pittsburgh.
    htm.

17. R. L. Duffus, "Is Pittsburgh civilized?" *Harper's
    Magazine*, October 1930.

18. "Our Big Cities Today and Tomorrow," *Wall
    Street Journal* 1944, as referred to by Robert C.
    Alberts in *The Shaping of the Point: Pittsburgh's
    Renaissance Park* (Pittsburgh: University of
    Pittsburgh Press, 1980), 58.

19. Dan Fitzpatrick, "The Story of Urban Renewal,"
    Pittsburgh Post-Gazette, May 21, 2000.

20. Clarke M. Thomas, narrative for *Witness to the
    Fifties: The Pittsburgh Photographic Library,
    1950–1953*, edited by Constance B. Schulz and
    Steven W. Plattners (Pittsburgh: University of
    Pittsburgh Press, 1999), 48–50.

21. Point State Park was designed by landscape
    architect Ralph Griswold and architect
    Charles M. Stotz, in collaboration with Clarke
    + Rapuano (who also did the site plan for the
    adjacent Gateway Center). The park was con-
    structed between 1954 and 1974, and renovated
    from 2007–2013, based on a plan by Pressley
    Associates.

22. David L. Lawrence, "The Point: Mayor
    Lawrence on Urban Design," *Charette* 36/5
    (May 1956). Excerpts from address delivered
    at a conference on urban design, hosted by
    Harvard University's Graduate School of
    Design, organized by Dean Jose Louis Sert.

23. The regional planning organization initially
    formed in 1943 was named the "Citizens
    Sponsoring Committee of Postwar Planning
    for the Metropolitan Area of Allegheny County."
    The organization was soon renamed the
    Allegheny Conference on Post War Community
    Planning, which was ultimately shortened
    the Allegheny Conference on Community
    Development in 1944.

24. Lubove, *Twentieth-Century Pittsburgh*, 126.

25. Ibid.

26. Mitchell, Ritchey, and Richardson, *Parking Park
    Study*.

27. The interior is now in the permanent collection
    of the Victoria and Albert Museum, given by
    Edgar Kaufmann Jr. in 1974.

28. Richard Cleary, "Edgar J. Kaufmann, Frank Lloyd Wright and the 'Pittsburgh Point Park Coney Island in Automobile Scale,'" *Journal of the Society of Architectural Historians* 52/2 (June 1993): 139–158.

29. According to Marjorie Simonds, in a 2008 interview with Patricia O'Donnell, Simonds and Dahlen Ritchey were key figures in this effort, although the accompanying exhibition booklet does not credit Simonds & Simonds.

30. Mitchell and Ritchey, *Pittsburgh in Progress*.

31. Martin Aurand, *The Spectator and the Topographical City* (Pittsburgh: University of Pittsburgh Press, 2006), 56–57.

32. Allen Freeman, "Where the People Are: In Pittsburgh, A Work in Progress and A Work of Enduring Popularity," *Landscape Architecture* 93/7 (July 2003): 135.

33. Pittsburgh History and Landmarks Foundation, *Whirlwind Walk: Architecture and Urban Spaces in Downtown Pittsburgh* (Pittsburgh: Pittsburgh History and Landmarks Foundation, 2011), 35.

34. The Mellon fortune was built on banking, beginning with Scotch-Irish immigrant Thomas Mellon, who arrived at age 5 in 1818. A lawyer, he started a private bank, T. Mellon & Sons, in 1869. Early investments in real estate development and in coal through Henry Clay Frick and Andrew Carnegie created the first generation of wealth, which was then invested in launching a vast array of enterprises involving aluminum, silicon carbide, oil, steel, shipbuilding, and railroads.

35. "Mellons Donate $4 million Gift for Triangle Park," *Pittsburgh Post-Gazette*, April 24, 1949.

36. David T. Jones, "Mellons Give City 4 Millions for Park, Garage Downtown," *Pittsburgh Sun-Telegraph*, April 24, 1949.

37. "Pittsburgh Rebuilds," *Fortune* 45 (June 1952): 88–97.

38. John Mauro, "Magnificent Square in the Triangle," *Greater Pittsburgh* 37 (October 1955), 19–22, 62–63.

39. Jones, *Pittsburgh Sun-Telegraph*.

40. Richard K. Mellon, remarks at the dedication of Mellon Square Park, October 18, 1955, (Library and Archives Division, Historical Society of Western Pennsylvania, Heinz History Center).

41. Richard K. Mellon, remarks at the groundbreaking of Mellon Square Park, September 28, 1953, (Library and Archives Division, Historical Society of Western Pennsylvania, Heinz History Center).

42. See Stefan Lorant, *Pittsburgh: The Story of an American City* (Garden City, NY: Doubleday and Company, Inc., 1964), 364–65, 374–75.

43. John O. Simonds, "Mellon Square: An Oasis in an Asphalt Desert," *Landscape Architecture Quarterly* 58/3 (July 1958): 208–11.

Chapter 3:
Concepts and Ideas for Mellon Square, 1949–1955

1. Mauro, "Magnificent Square in the Triangle," 1955.

2. Ibid. Mellon's aide Wallace Richards approached the firm on the Friday before Labor Day in 1949 and asked for the drawings by Tuesday morning.

3. Project notes, ca. late 1940s, EP&D archives, Pittsburgh.

4. Freeman, "Where the People Are," 135.

5. Howard B. Stewart, Director of the Department of Parks and Recreation, City of Pittsburgh, to Ralph W. Olmstead, Morrison-Knudson Company, April 9, 1952.

6. Ibid.

7. Ibid.

8. Ibid.

9. Ibid.

10. Ibid.

11. "Conversation between R. Olmstead, Morrison-Knudsen, and Mitchell and Ritchey," April 16, 1952, EP&D Archives, Pittsburgh.

12. Mauro, "The Magnificent Square in the Triangle," 1955.

13. John O. Simonds to Mitchell & Ritchey, May 10, 1955, EP&D Archives, Pittsburgh.

14. Frank Curto, "Mellon Square Park," *Brooklyn Botanic Garden Record*, 33.

15. "Fabulous Mellon Park Opens Tuesday," *Pittsburgh Press*, October 16, 1955.

16. "Mellon Square's Roof Really Built to Last," *Pittsburgh Press*, October 16, 1955.

Chapter 4:
Elevating the Square: Platform, Trees, and Water

1. Simonds, "Mellon Square: An Oasis in an Asphalt Desert," 208–12.

2. Ibid.

3. Freeman, "Where the People Are," 135.

4. Simonds & Simonds would also employ this tile pattern in the design of Equitable Plaza.

5. Heritage Landscapes, *Mellon Square*, 10.

6. This isolated area had been envisioned as a terrace in plans shown as part of the 1947 Pittsburgh in Progress exhibit at Kaufmann's Department Store.

7. "Philip is a born innovator, always frigging around in an effort to do it simpler and better." See John O. Simonds, "Community Planning and Design," (address to 1982 Annual Meeting, PA/DEL Chapter of ASLA, Hyatt Pittsburgh, PA, April 17, 1982).

8. Robert Vukich and Melissa Marshall, MTR Landscape Architects, interview with the author, July 7, 2009. MTR is a spin-off firm from EP&D.

9. *Whirlwind Walk: Architecture and Urban Spaces in Downtown Pittsburgh* (Pittsburgh: Pittsburgh History & Landmarks Foundation, 2011), 35.

10. Heritage Landscapes, *Mellon Square*, 19.

11. John O. Simonds, "Community Planning and Design" (address, Annual Meeting of PA/DE Chapter ASLA, Hyatt Hotel, Pittsburgh, PA, April 17, 1982).

12. Heritage Landscapes, *Mellon Square*, 12.

Chapter 5:
Lifecycles

1. "Mellon Square Park Due to Open at 12:30 p.m.," *Pittsburgh Post-Gazette*, October 18, 1955.

2. "Mellon Square Park Turned Over to City," *Pittsburgh Post-Gazette*, October 19, 1955.

3. "Mellon Square, General Information," Allegheny Conference on Community Development, October 1955.

4. Ibid.

5. "Mellon Park Transforms Area," *Pittsburgh Post-Gazette,* October 18, 1955.

6. "Mellon Square Shops Unique," *Pittsburgh Post-Gazette*, October 18, 1955.

7. John Mauro, "Magnificent Square in the Triangle," *Charette* 35/12 (Pittsburgh: Pittsburgh Architectural Club, December 1955): 13–16. Reprinted from *Greater Pittsburgh*, October 1955.

8. Ralph E. Griswold to Richard King Mellon, October 21, 1955 (Pittsburgh: Library and Archives Division, Historical Society of Western Pennsylvania, Heinz History Center).

9. Ralph E. Griswold to Mitchell & Ritchey, October 21, 1955 (Pittsburgh: Library and Archives Division, Historical Society of Western Pennsylvania, Heinz History Center).

10. "Statement of Record" regarding the advertisement in *Pittsburgh Press* "Pittsburgh Renaissance" supplement and related advertisement copy, December 13 and 14, 1953 (Pittsburgh: Library and Archives Division, Historical Society of Western Pennsylvania, Heinz History Center).

11. *Pittsburgh Press* to John O. Simonds, December 23, 1953 (Pittsburgh: Library and Archives Division, Historical Society of Western Pennsylvania, Heinz History Center).

12. Ralph Griswold to John O. Simonds, December 17, 1953 (Pittsburgh: Library and Archives Division, Historical Society of Western Pennsylvania, Heinz History Center).

13. Marjorie Simonds, interview.

14. Philip Simonds, "The Birth of a Regional Park System," 206–8.

15. *Pittsburgh and Allegheny County: An Era of Progress and Accomplishment*, (Pittsburgh: Allegheny Conference on Community Development, September 1956).

16. John Grove, "Pittsburgh—The Renaissance City," *Greater Pittsburgh* (Summer 1973).

17. Jane Jacobs, "Downtown is for People," *Fortune* (July 1958).

18. "Mellon Square Policy Statement," February 6, 1956, (Heinz History Center, ACCD Box 136-F5.)

19. Department of Parks and Recreation Director Robert J. Templeton to the President and Members of Council, Pittsburgh, PA, March 26, 1959.

20. Sixteen stainless steel tubes are linked by cables to form a freestanding structure that is regarded as a superb example of the American sculptor Kenneth Snelson's compositions of rigid and flexible components, which he has termed "floating compression." A series of conversations led by the Pittsburgh Parks Conservancy from 2009–13 among stakeholders (including the Carnegie Museum of Art, the city, and the Office of Public Art) achieved an agreement for the Carnegie Museum to remove the Snelson sculpture from Mellon Square and relocate it to museum grounds, in accordance with the recommendation of the *Mellon Square Preservation, Interpretation and Management Plan* to restore the original intent of a forest-like composition to this planting bed.

21. City Horticulturist Ed Vasilcik to Louise R. Brown, director of Parks and Recreation, June 15, 1978.

22. "Pittsburgh: History," City Data, accessed November 2013, www.city-data.com/us-cities/The-Northeast/Pittsburgh-History.html.

23. Louise R. Brown to Robert B. Burr Jr., Secretary of the Richard King Mellon Foundation, April 13, 1981 (Pittsburgh: Library and Archives Division, Historical Society of Western Pennsylvania, Heinz History Center).

24. Environmental Planning & Design, "Mellon
    Square Improvements," (Pittsburgh: Allegheny
    Conference on Community Development,
    1983). Commissioned with the support of the
    Richard King Mellon Foundation.
25. Ibid.
26. Bob Vukich interview with the author,
    September 3, 2013.
27. Marjorie Simonds, interview.
28. EP&D, "Mellon Square Improvements."
29. Ibid.
30. Paul Farmer, Department of City Planning, to
    Paul Wolfe, EP&D, May 19, 1983 (Pittsburgh:
    Library and Archives Division, Historical
    Society of Western Pennsylvania, Heinz History
    Center).
31. Ibid.
32. Ibid.
33. Jonathan Barnett to David Bergholz,
    September 3, 1982 (Pittsburgh: Library
    and Archives Division, Historical Society of
    Western Pennsylvania, Heinz History Center).
34. Paul J. McDermott, Department of Engineering
    and Construction, to Paul Wolfe, EP&D,
    November 1, 1985.
35. Bob Vukich interview with the author,
    September 20, 2013.

Chapter 6:
The Future of Mellon Square

1. The team included: Robert Silman Associates
    (structural engineering), Grenald Waldron
    Associates (lighting), and Neil Silberman
    (interpretive planning). Key partners included
    The Cultural Landscape Foundation, Pittsburgh
    Downtown Partnership, Pittsburgh History and
    Landmarks Foundation, City of Pittsburgh, and
    PPA.
2. Mellon Square is listed as a contributing
    feature to the "Midtown Business District"
    listing in the National Register. Mellon Square
    is strongly eligible as a premiere example of the
    national urban renewal movement, Pittsburgh's
    Renaissance I, and a modern designed urban
    landscape in the city's downtown central
    business district. It is significant as the first
    Modernist garden plaza built over a parking
    structure, the third park constructed over such
    a structure in the United States and, unlike its
    predecessors, survives with a high degree of
    integrity. It also presents an early example of
    sustainability with its innovative "green" roof.
    Its association with the lives of significant
    persons including David L. Lawrence and R.

    K. Mellon is another eligibility factor. Mellon
    Square represents a dynamic collabora-
    tion between recognized master landscape
    architects Simonds & Simonds and leading
    Pittsburgh architects Mitchell & Ritchey.
    The plaza possesses high artistic value as an
    expression of Modernist design in an urban
    civic gathering space, engaging in form, tex-
    ture, detail, and relationship with surrounding
    buildings.
3. Charles A. Birnbaum and Christine Capella
    Peters, *Secretary of the Interior's Standards
    for the Treatment of Historic Properties with
    Guidelines for the Treatment of Cultural
    Landscapes* (Washington, D.C.: National
    Park Service, 1998). See also *A Guide to
    Cultural Landscape Reports: Contents, Process,
    and Techniques, and National Park Service
    Director's Order #28: Cultural Resource
    Management* (National Park Service).
4. Heritage Landscapes, *Mellon Square
    Preservation, Interpretation & Management
    Plan*, 2009, 10:3.
5. Birnbaum and Peters, *Secretary of the Interior's
    Standards for the Treatment of Historic
    Properties with Guidelines for the Treatment of
    Cultural Landscapes*.
6. Ibid.
7. Ibid.
8. Ibid.
9. Ibid.
10. Neil A. Silberman is an archaeologist and histo-
    rian specializing in public heritage interpreta-
    tion and presentation, who served as a member
    of the 2009 planning team for Mellon Square.
11. Charles Birnbaum, "Mellon Square: A
    Nationally Significant Public Space."
12. 4Ward Planning, "Mellon Square Economic
    Analysis" and "Mellon Square Revenue-
    Generation Opportunities," (Pittsburgh:
    Pittsburgh Parks Conservancy, 2010).
13. The renovation project design team was
    led by Heritage Landscapes, with Atlantic
    Engineering Services, Allen & Shariff
    Engineering, Pfaffmann and Associates
    (architecture), Hilbish McGee Lighting Design,
    and MORTAR & ink (graphic design). Parks
    Curator Susan Rademacher of the Pittsburgh
    Parks Conservancy, served as project manager
    for the design phase; construction was man-
    aged by Phil Gruszka, the Conservancy's
    director of parks maintenance and manage-
    ment, and Jim Griffin, director of facilities for
    the Conservancy.

14. Matthews designed and built an ingenious sloped rotating stand to accommodate the crew while sandblasting and applying a new drip edge. Michael Kraus, an independent sculptor, and his associate Bill Williams, performed the patinating.

15. Meg Cheever, President and CEO, Pittsburgh Parks Conservancy, as quoted in the video, *Mellon Square: An American Masterpiece* (Pittsburgh: Pittsburgh Parks Conservancy, 2010).

16. James van Trump, *Life and Architecture in Pittsburgh* (Pittsburgh: Pittsburgh History and Landmarks Foundation, 1983), 18.

Epilogue: John O. Simonds: Philosopher, Author, Educator

1. John O. Simonds to Barry W. Starke, ca. 1998.

2. American Society of Landscape Architects news release (Washington, D.C.: American Society of Landscape Architects, ca. September 15, 1999).

3. Simonds, *Landscape Architecture*, 1961; Urban Advisors to the Federal Highway Administration (Michael Rapuano, Lawrence Halprin, Thomas C. Kavanagh, Harry R. Powell, Kevin Roche, Matthew L. Rockwell, John O. Simonds, Marvin R. Springer), *The Freeway in the City: Principles of Planning and Design*, Report to the Secretary of Transportation, (Washington, D.C.: U.S. Government Printing Office, 1968.); Simonds, *Garden Cities* 21, 1994; Simonds, *Earthscape*, 1978.

4. Sara Katherine (Kay) Williams in "One Life, Many Lessons: Remembrances and Appreciations of John O. Simonds (1913–2005)," *Landscape Architecture* (September 2005): 108–10.

5. J. Todd Simonds in "One Life, Many Lessons: Remembrances and Appreciations of John O. Simonds (1913–2005)," *Landscape Architecture* (September 2005): 103.

Appendix

1. Roy Lubove, *Twentieth-Century Pittsburgh: Government, Business, and Environmental Change,* (New York: John Wiley & Sons, Inc., 1969), 126.

2. "Mellon Square Park Turned Over to City," *Pittsburgh Post-Gazette*, October 18, 1955.

3. John Grove, "Pittsburgh—The Renaissance City," *Greater Pittsburgh Magazine,* Summer 1973.

4. City of Pittsburgh, "Mayor Announces Renovation of Mellon Square Park," press release, undated, MSS285.B312.F4, Library and Archives Division, Historical Society of Western Pennsylvania, Pittsburgh, PA.

5. Paul J. McDermott, Department of Engineering and Construction, City of Pittsburgh to Paul Wolfe, EP&D, November 1, 1985, EP&D.

Appendix

Plant List: 1955, 1989, 2013

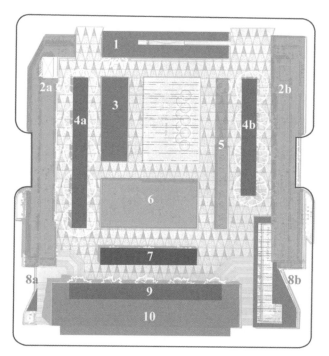

William Penn Place

6th Avenue

Oliver Avenue

Smithfield Street

1955

1

Fagus sylvatica (European beech)
Hedera helix 'Gracilis' (English ivy)
Hedera helix 'Hahns Maple Queen' (Hahn's Maple Queen ivy)
Ilex c. 'Green Island' (stokes holly)
Pieris japonica (Japanese andromeda)
Pyracantha c. 'Lanlandi' (scarlet firethorn)
Sophora japonica (Japanese pagoda tree)

2a | 2b

(Assorted annuals)
Aronia arbutifolia 'Brilliantissima' (red chokeberry)
Berberis julianae (wintergreen barberry)
Euonymus fortunei 'Coloratus' (purpleleaf euonymus)
Hedera helix 'Baltica' (Baltic ivy)
Hedera helix 'Hahns Green Ripple' (Hahn's Green Ripple ivy)
Hedera helix 'Hahns Maple Queen' (Hahn's Maple Queen ivy)
Ilex c. 'Green Island' (stokes holly)
Ilex c. 'Rotundifolia' (roundleaf Japanese holly)
Pieris floribunda (mountain pieris)
Pyracantha c. 'Lanlandi' (scarlet firethorn)
Rhododendron hybrid (red rhododendron)
Rhododendron smirnowii (Boursault rhododendron)
Tilia cordata (littleleaf linden)

3

Magnolia virginiana (sweetbay magnolia)
Pachysandra terminalis (pachysandra)

4a | 4b

Gleditzia triacanthos var. *inermis* (honey locust)
Hedera helix 'Baltica' (Baltic ivy)
Ilex c. 'Convexa' (convexleaf holly)

5

(Assorted annuals)
Hedera helix 'Gracilis' (English ivy)
Magnolia × soulangiana 'Lennei' (saucer magnolia)

6

Hedera helix 'Hahns Maple Queen' (Hahn's Maple Queen ivy)
Pinus Mugo (waterer Scotch pine)
Stewartia ovata var. *grandiflora* (mountain stewartia)

7

Hedera helix 'Hahns Green Ripple' (Hahn's Green Ripple ivy)
Malus 'Dolgo' (zumi crab)
Pieris japonica (Japanese andromeda)

8a | 8b

(Assorted annuals)
Hedera helix 'Baltica' (Baltic ivy)
Hedera helix 'Hahns Maple Queen' (Hahn's Maple Queen ivy)
Ilex c. 'Green Island' (stokes holly)
Ilex c. 'Rotundifolia' (roundleaf Japanese holly)
Ligustrum × ibolium (imbolium privet)
Malus baccata columnaris (columnar crab)
Malus purpurea eleyi (eley purple crab)
Pieris floribunda (mountain pieris)

9

Azalea ledifolia (azalea)
Berberis julianae (wintergreen barberry)
Ilex c. 'Green Island' (stokes holly)
Tilia tomentosa (silver linden)

10

Aronia arbutifolia 'Brilliantissima' (red chokeberry)
Azalea ledifolia (azalea)
Azalea o. 'Amoena' (azalea)
Franklinia alatamaha (Franklinia)
Hedera helix 'Baltica' (Baltic ivy)
Ilex c. 'Convexa' (box)
Ilex c. 'Rotundifolia' (roundleaf Japanese holly)
Rhododendron roseum elegans (pink rhodendron)
Taxus m. 'Hicksii' (yew)
Viburnum p. tomentosum 'Mariesii' (Maries doublefire viburnum)

1987

1

(Assorted annuals)
Fagus sylvatica (European beech)
Narcissus 'Duke of Windsor' ('Duke of Windsor' daffodils)
Narcissus 'Ice Follies' ('Ice Follies' daffodils)
Sophora japonica (Japanese pagoda tree)
Taxus baccata (Serbian yew)
Viburnum × *juddii* (Judd's viburnum)

2a | 2b

(Assorted annuals)
Aronia melanocarpa (black chokeberry)
Euonymus fortunei 'Greenlane' ('Greenlane' wintercreeper)
Magnolia stellata (star magnolia)
Narcissus 'Unsurpassable' ('Unsurpassable' daffodil)
Pachysandra terminalis 'Green Carpet' ('Green Carpet' pachysandra)
Rhododendron maximum (rosebay rhododendron)
Stephanandra incisa 'Crispa' ('Crispa' lace shrub)
Taxus × *media* 'Chadwickii' ('Chadwickii' yew)
Taxus × *media* 'Densiformis' ('Densiformis' yew)
Taxus × *media* 'Everlow' ('Everlow' yew)
Tilia cordata 'Greenspire' ('Greenspire' littleleaf linden)
Viburnum carlesii (Korean spice viburnum)
Viburnum × *juddii* (Judd's viburnum)

3

Magnolia virginiana (sweetbay magnolia)
Narcissus 'Duke of Windsor' ('Duke of Windsor' daffodils)
Narcissus 'Ice Follies' ('Ice Follies' daffodils)
Pachysandra terminalis 'Green Carpet' ('Green Carpet' pachysandra)

4a | 4b

Gleditsia triacanthos var. *inermis* 'Halka' ('Halka' thornless honey locust)
Pachysandra terminalis 'Green Carpet' ('Green Carpet' pachysandra)

5

(Assorted annuals)
Buxus sempervirens 'Vadar Valley' ('Vadar Valley' boxwood)
Magnolia × *soulangiana* 'Lennei' ('Lennei' saucer magnolia)

Pachysandra terminalis 'Green Carpet' ('Green Carpet' pachysandra)
Taxus × *media* 'Brownii' ('Brownii' yew)

6

Athletic turf

7

(Assorted annuals)
Buxus sempervirens 'Vadar Valley' ('Vadar Valley' boxwood)
Malus 'Donald Wyman' ('Donald Wyman' crabapple)
Pachysandra terminalis 'Green Carpet' ('Green Carpet' pachysandra)
Taxus × *media* 'Hatfieldii' ('Hatfieldii' yew)

8a | 8b

(Assorted annuals)
Euonymus alatus 'Compactus' ('Compactus' dwarf burning bush)
Ilex glabra 'Nordic' ('Nordic' holly)
Magnolia × *loebneri* 'Merrill' ('Merrill' magnolia)
Pachysandra terminalis 'Green Carpet' ('Green Carpet' pachysandra)
Stephanandra incisa 'Crispa' ('Crispa' lace shrub)
Taxus × *media* 'Chadwickii' ('Chadwickii' yew)

9

Liquidambar styraciflua (American sweetgum)
Pachysandra terminalis 'Green Carpet' ('Green Carpet' pachysandra)

10

Euonymus alatus 'Compactus' ('Compactus' dwarf burning bush)
Pachysandra terminalis 'Green Carpet' ('Green Carpet' pachysandra)
Parrotia persica (Persian ironwood)
Rhododendron 'Boudoir' ('Boudoir' azalea)
Rhododendron maximum ('Pink Maxima' rhododendron)
Taxus baccata (Serbian yew)
Taxus × *media* 'Chadwickii' ('Chadwickii' yew)
Viburnum plicatum 'Newzam' ('Newzam' Newport doublefire virburnum)

2013

1

Arctostaphylos uva-ursi (common bearberry)
Carpinus fastigiata (pyramidal hophornbeam)
Cornus kousa (Korean dogwood)
Pachysandra terminalis (pachysandra)
Spiraea betulifolia 'Tor' ('Tor' birchleaf spirea)
Taxus × media 'Everlow' ('Everlow' yew)
Viburnum × burkwoodii 'Mohawk' ('Mohawk'
    viburnum)
Viburnum × juddii (Judd's viburnum)

2a | 2b

Aronia arbutifolia (chokeberry)
Euonymus fortune 'Coloratus' ('Coloratus'
    wintergreen euonymus)
Gautheria procumbens 'Red Baron' ('Red Baron'
    creeping wintergreen)
Ilex glabra 'Compacta' ('Compacta' inkberry holly)
Rhododendron 'Girard Pleasant White' ('Girard
    Pleasant White' azalea)
Stephanandra incisa 'Crispa' ('Crispa' lace shrub)
Tilia cordata (littleleaf linden)
Viburnum × juddii (Judd's viburnum)

3

Allium (ornamental onion)
Magnolia virginiana (sweetbay magnolia)
Narcissus (daffodils)
Pachysandra terminalis (pachysandra)
Tulipa (tulips)

4a | 4b

Hedera helix 'Baltica' ('Baltica' ivy)
Ilex glabra 'Compacta' ('Compacta' inkberry holly)
Parrotia persica (Persian ironwood)

5

Artemesia schmidtiana 'Silver Mound' ('Silver
    Mound' artemesia)
Buxus × 'Green Mound' ('Green Mound' boxwood)
Coreopsis grandiflora 'Sundancer' ('Sundancer'
    coreopsis)
Lavandula angustifolia 'Thumbelina Leigh'
    ('Thumbelina Leigh' lavender)

6

Allium (ornamental onion)
Chamaemelum nobile (chamomile)
Cotinus obovatus (American smoketree)

Gaultheria procumbens (creeping wintergreen)
Mentha pulegium 'Nana' ('Nana' mint)
Narcissus (daffodils)
Pinus bungeana (lacebark pine)
Pinus cembra (swiss stone pine)
Pinus mugo (mugo pine)
Tulipa (tulips)

7

Arctostaphylos uva-ursi (common bearberry)
Malus 'Donald Wyman' ('Donald Wyman' crabapple)
Spiraea betulifolia 'Tor' ('Tor' birchleaf spirea)

8a | 8b

(Assorted annuals)
Arctostophylos uva-ursi (common bearberry)
Gautheria procumbens 'Red Baron' ('Red Baron'
    creeping wintergreen)
Hedera helix 'Baltica' ('Baltica' ivy)
Ilex glabra 'Compacta' ('Compacta' inkberry holly)
Malus 'Donald Wyman' ('Donald Wyman' crabapple)
Spiraea betulifolia 'Tor' ('Tor' birchleaf spirea)
Taxus × media 'Everlow' ('Everlow' yew)

9

Buxus × 'Green Mound' ('Green Mound' boxwood)
Rhododendron 'Girard Pleasant White' ('Girard
    Pleasant White' azalea)
Tilia tomentosa (silver leaf linden)

10

Engineered lawn
Amalanchier canadensis 'Robin Hill' ('Robin Hill'
    serviceberry)
Buxus × 'Green Mound' ('Green Mound' boxwood)
Hedera helix 'Baltica' ('Baltica' Thorndale ivy)
Rhododendron 'Girard Pleasant White' ('Girard
    Pleasant White' azalea)
Sedum album 'Coral Carpet' ('Coral Carpet'
    stonecrop)
Sedum floriferum 'Weihenstephaner Gold'
    ('Weihenstephaner Gold' stonecrop)
Sedum hybridum 'Immergrunchen' ('Immergrunchen'
    stonecrop)
Sedum reflexum (stonecrop)
Sedum rupestre 'Angelina' ('Angelina' stonecrop)
Sedum sexanglare (stonecrop)
Sedum spurium 'Dragon's Blood' ('Dragon's Blood'
    stonecrop)
Sedum spurium 'Voo Doo' ('Voo Doo' stonecrop)
Taxus × media 'Tauntonii' ('Tauntonii' yew)
Viburnum × burkwoodii 'Conoy' ('Conoy' viburnum)
Viburnum plicatum f. tomentosum 'Mariesii'
    ('Mariesii' doublefile viburnum)

Selected Bibliography

Alberts, Robert C. *The Shaping of the Point: Pittsburgh's Renaissance Park.* Pittsburgh: University of Pittsburgh Press, 1981. http://digital.library.pitt.edu/cgi-bin/t/text/text-idx?id no=31735039418946;view=toc;c=pittpress.

Allegheny Conference on Community Development Presents...Pittsburgh and Allegheny County: An Era of Progress and Accomplishment. Pittsburgh: Allegheny Conference on Community Development, 1956.

Andrews, David. "Surviving Steel: Pittsburgh in the Post-Industrial Era." *Common Ground* (Fall 2006): 34–45.

Aurand, Martin. "Mitchell & Ritchey Collection." Carnegie Mellon University Architecture Archives, Pittsburgh.

———. *The Spectator and the Topographical City.* Pittsburgh: University of Pittsburgh Press, 2006.

Baldwin, Leland D. *Pittsburgh, The Story of a City: 1750–1865.* Pittsburgh: University of Pittsburgh Press, 1937. Digital Editions, http://digital.library.pitt.edu/cac he/1/3/1/7/31735039418946/0001.jp2.S.jpg.

Birnbaum, Charles A., ed. *Pioneers of American Landscape Design.* New York: McGraw-Hill, 2000.

———, ed. *Preserving Modern Landscape Architecture I: Proceedings from the Wave Hill Conference.* Cambridge, MA: Spacemaker Press, 1999.

———, ed. *Shaping the American Landscape: New Profiles from the Pioneers of American Landscape Design Project.* Charlottesville: University of Virginia Press, 2009.

———, ed. with Jane Gillette and Nancy Slade. *Preserving Modern Landscape Architecture II: Making Postwar Landscape Visible.* Washington, D.C.: Spacemaker Press, 2004.

———, and Christine Capella Peters. *Secretary of the Interior's Standards for the Treatment of Historic Properties with Guidelines for the Treatment of Cultural Landscapes.* Washington, D.C.: National Park Service, 1998. See also *A Guide to Cultural Landscape Reports: Contents, Process,* and *Techniques, and National Park Service Director's Order #28: Cultural Resource Management* (National Park Service).

Cleary, Richard L. "Edgar J. Kaufmann, Frank Lloyd Wright and the 'Pittsburgh Point Park Coney Island in Automobile Scale.'" *Journal of the Society of Architectural Historians* 52, no. 2 (1993): 139–58.

———. *Merchant Prince and Master Builder: Edgar J. Kaufmann and Frank Lloyd Wright.* Pittsburgh: Heinz Architectural Center, 1999.

Cook, Laura. "Restoration of Historic Mellon Square." *Pennsylvania Recreation & Parks* (First Quarter, 2010): 32–38.

Curto, Frank. "Mellon Square Park." *Carnegie Magazine* 33/6 (June 1959): 185–92. Reprinted from *Brooklyn Botanic Garden Record/Plants & Gardens/Handbook on Gardening* 15/1 (Spring 1959).

Demorest, Rose. "Pittsburgh: A Bicentennial Tribute 1758–1958." Pittsburgh: Carnegie Library of Pittsburgh, 1958. http://www.clpgh.org/research/pittsburgh/history/demorest.html.

Downtown: A Golden Triangle. Pittsburgh: University of Pittsburgh Press, 2009.

Duffus, R. L. "Is Pittsburgh Civilized?" *Harper's Magazine* 161 (October 1930): 537–45.

Economou, Bessie C. *Forging the Pittsburgh Renaissance.* Pittsburgh: Urban Redevelopment Authority of Pittsburgh, 1997.

Emanuel, Muriel, ed. Contemporary Architects. 3rd ed. Detroit: St. James Press, 1994.

Environmental Planning & Design. *Mellon Square Improvements.* Pittsburgh: Allegheny Conference on Community Development, 1983.

Freeman, Allen. "Where the People Are: In Pittsburgh, A Work in Progress and A Work of Enduring Popularity." *Landscape Architecture* 93/7 (July 2003): 135.

Griswold, Ralph E. "From Fort Pitt to Point Park: A Turning Point in the Physical Planning of Pittsburgh." *Landscape Architecture* 46 (July 1956).

Grove, John. "Pittsburgh—The Renaissance City." *Greater Pittsburgh* (Summer 1973).

Heritage Landscapes. *Mellon Square: Preservation, Interpretation & Management Plan.* With contributions by Grenald Waldron Associates, RSA Associates, and Neil Silberman. Pittsburgh: Pittsburgh Parks Conservancy, 2009.

Hopper, Justin. "Full Circle for the Square." *Pittsburgh Quarterly* (Fall 2009): 50–56, 148–149.

Jacobs, Jane. "Downtown is for People." *Fortune* (1958). http://features.blogs.fortune.cnn.com/2011/09/18/downtown-is-for-people-fortune-classic-1958/.

John Ormsbee Simonds Collection, Special and Area Studies Collections, George A. Smathers Libraries, University of Florida, Gainesville, Florida. http://www.uflib.ufl.edu/spec/manuscript/guides/simonds.htm.

"John Ormsbee Simonds Remembered: Visionary landscape Architect, Planner, Educator, and Environmentalist (1913–2005)." University of Florida, George A. Smathers Libraries. Exhibition catalog, November 15, 2005–February 3, 2006.

Killikelly, Sarah Hutchins. *The History of Pittsburgh: Its Rise and Progress.* Pittsburgh: B. C. & Gordon Montgomery Company, 1906.

Lawrence, David L. "The Point: Mayor Lawrence on Urban Design." *Charette* 36/5 (May 1956).

Leccese, Michael. "Mystical Pragmatist." *Landscape Architecture* 80/3 (March 1990): 78–83.

Leighton, Henry. *The Geology of Pittsburgh and its Environs.* Pittsburgh: Carnegie Museum, 1927.

Lorant, Stefan. *Pittsburgh: The Story of an American City.* Garden City, NY: Doubleday and Company, 1964.

Lubove, Roy. *Twentieth-Century Pittsburgh: Government, Business and Environmental Change.* New York: John Wiley & Sons, 1969.

——. *Twentieth-Century Pittsburgh: The Post-Steel Era,* Volume II. Pittsburgh: University of Pittsburgh Press, 1996.

Mann, William A. *Landscape Architecture: An Illustrated History in Timelines, Site Plans, and Biography.* New York: John Wiley and Sons, 1993.

Mauro, John. "Magnificent Square in the Triangle." *Greater Pittsburgh,* 37 (October 1955): 19–22, 62–63.

"Mellon Square Park." *Carnegie Magazine* 33 (June 1959), 185–89.

"Mellon's Miracle: The Head of Pittsburgh's First Family Leads His City into a Renaissance," *Life* 40:20 (May 14, 1956).

Miller, Randall M., and William Pencak, eds. *Pennsylvania: A History of the Commonwealth.* University Park, PA: Pennsylvania State University Press, 2002.

Mitchell & Ritchey, "Brochure on Background and Qualifications." Ca. 1955. Courtesy of Edward Mitchell.

——, and George S. Richardson. *Parking Park Study: A City Park and Underground Parking Garage for Pittsburgh's Golden Triangle.* Pittsburgh: Regional Planning Authority, 1949.

Mitchell, James A., and L. Grant. "An Open Place at the Heart of a City." *Architectural Record* 121 (February 1957).

——, and Dahlen K. Ritchey. *Pittsburgh in Progress.* Pittsburgh: Kaufmann's, 1947.

——, "Impressions and Reflections." *Charette* 17:7 (July 1937), 1–2; 17:8 (August 1937), 1–2.

Muller, Edward K. "Downtown Pittsburgh: Renaissance and Renewal." In *Pittsburgh and the Appalachians: Cultural and Natural Resources in a Postindustrial Age,* edited by Joseph L. Scarpaci with Kevin J. Patrick, 7–19. Pittsburgh: University of Pittsburgh Press, 2006.

National Register of Historic Places. "Allegheny Commons." Washington, D.C.: National Park Service, 2013.

——. "Pittsburgh Central Downtown Historic District." Washington, D.C.: National Park Service, 2013.

Northside Leadership Conference. *Allegheny Commons Master Plan.* Prepared by Pressley Associates. Pittsburgh: Northside Leadership Conference, 2002.

Pearlman, Jill E. *Inventing American Modernism: Joseph Hudnut, Walter Gropius, and the Bauhaus Legacy at Harvard.* Charlottesville: University of Virginia Press, 2007.

Pennsylvania Historical & Museum Commission. "Late Woodland Period in the Susquehanna and Delaware River Valley." http://www.portal.state.pa.us/portal/server.pt/community/native_american_archaearcha/3316/late_woodland_period/406837.

Pittsburgh and Allegheny County: An Era of Progress and Accomplishment. Pittsburgh: Allegheny Conference on Community Development, September 1956.

Pittsburgh History & Landmarks Foundation. *Downtown Pittsburgh Grant Street Walking Tour.* Pittsburgh: Pittsburgh History & Landmarks Foundation. 2013.

——. *Whirlwind Walk: Architecture and Urban Spaces in Downtown Pittsburgh.* Pittsburgh: Pittsburgh History & Landmarks Foundation, 2011.

Pittsburgh Post-Gazette. "A Pittsburgh Century." *Interactive Edition of the Pittsburgh Post-Gazette.* http://www.post-gazette.com/newslinks/timeline1981.asp.

"Pittsburgh Rebuilds." *Fortune* 45 (June 1952).

"Pittsburgh Renascent: Two New Skyscrapers of Smart, Clean Design will Flank a New Mid-City Park." *Architectural Forum* 91 (November 1949), 66–69, 110.

"Pittsburgh: History." City-Data. www.city-data.com/us-cities/The-Northeast/Pittsburgh-History.html.

Rademacher, Susan M. "Bringing the Glamour Back Downtown: Pittsburgh Revives Its Mellon Square." *Forum/Larrimor's* (Spring 2012): 48–49.

———. "Reviving the Square in the Heart of the Triangle." In "Modern Landscape Architecture: Presentation and Preservation," Charles A. Birnbaum, ed. *Forum Journal* 27/2 (January 2013): 12–18. http://muse.jhu.edu/journals/forum_journal/toc/fmj.27.2.html.

Remington, Fred. "Architect of the Renaissance." *Pittsburgh* (October 1978): 38–41, 80–81.

Schulz, Constance B., and Steven W. Plattners, eds. *Witness to the Fifties: The Pittsburgh Photographic Library, 1950–1953.* Pittsburgh: University of Pittsburgh Press, 1999.

Simonds & Simonds. *Allegheny Commons: A Proposed Long-Range Development Plan.* April 1966.

Simonds, John O. "Equitable Plaza, Pittsburgh." *Landscape Architecture* 53:1 (October 1962), 18–19.

———. "Mellon Square: An Oasis in an Asphalt Desert." *Landscape Architecture* 48 (July 1958), 208–12.

———. *Earthscape: a Manual of Environmental Planning.* New York: Van Nostrand Reinhold, 1978.

———. *Garden Cities 21: Creating a Liveable Urban Environment.* New York: McGraw-Hill, 1994.

———. *Landscape Architecture: A Manual of Site Planning and Design.* New York: McGraw-Hill, 1961, 1983, 1997. Revised with Barry W. Starke, 2006, 2013.

———. *Lessons.* Washington, D.C.: ASLA Press, 1999.

———. *Vincent Lecture: Interview with Robinson Fisher.* Athens: University of Georgia School of Environmental Design, April 2, 1985. DVD. Hargrett Rare Book and Manuscript Library/University of Georgia Libraries.

Simonds, Philip D. "The Birth of a Regional Park System." *Landscape Architecture Quarterly* (April 1963): 206–8.

Starke, Barry W., J. Todd Simonds, Jack R. Scholl, Geoffrey Rausch, Samuel R. Hogue, Charles E. Turner, Sara Katherine Williams, et al. "One Life, Many Lessons: Remembrances and appreciations of John Ormsbee Simonds (1913–2005)," *Landscape Architecture* 95/9 (September 2005): 100–13.

Tannler, Albert M. *A List of Pittsburgh and Allegheny County Buildings and Architects, 1950–2005.* Pittsburgh: Pittsburgh History & Landmarks Foundation, 2005.

Tarr, Joel A., ed. *Devastation and Renewal: An Environmental History of Pittsburgh and Its Region.* Pittsburgh: University of Pittsburgh Press, 2003.

Thomas, Clarke. "Pittsburgh in the Fifties." *Common Ground* (Fall 2006): 20–33.

———. *Witness to the Fifties: The Pittsburgh Photographic Library, 1950–1953.* Pittsburgh: University of Pittsburgh Press, 1999.

Toker, Franklin. *Pittsburgh: A New Portrait.* Pittsburgh: University of Pittsburgh Press, 2009.

———. *Pittsburgh: An Urban Portrait.* University Park, PA: Pennsylvania State Press, 1986.

Treib, Marc, ed. *Modern Landscape Architecture: A Critical Review.* Cambridge, MA: MIT Press, 1993.

Urban Advisors to the Federal Highway Administration (Michael Rapuano, Lawrence Halprin, Thomas C. Kavanagh, Harry R. Powell, Kevin Roche, Matthew L. Rockwell, John O. Simonds, Marvin R. Springer), *The Freeway in the City: Principles of Planning and Design,* Report to the Secretary of Transportation, (Washington, D.C.: U.S. Government Printing Office, 1968.)

Van Trump, James. *Life and Architecture in Pittsburgh.* Pittsburgh: Pittsburgh History and Landmarks Foundation, 1983.

Walker, Peter, and Melanie Simo. *Invisible Gardens: The Search for Modernism in the American Landscape.* Cambridge, MA: MIT Press, 1996.

WQED. "Key Events in Pittsburgh History." http://www.wqed.org/erc/pghist/units/WPAhist/keyevents.htm .

Image Credits

Fig. 1, 4, 5, 14, 16, 17, 24, 28, 29, 30, 31, 32, 34, 42, 47, 48, 49, 53, 56, 57, 60, 62, 63, 64, 72, 73, 76, 78: Detre Library and Archives, Senator John Heinz History Center, Allegheny Conference on Community Development Collection

Fig. 2, 41, 45: Carnegie Mellon University Architectural Archives

Fig. 3: Harvard University Archives, UAV 605.270.1.2 (G-427)

Fig. 6, 13, 35, 36, 37, 38, 39, 40, 44, 50, 79, 81: Environmental Planning and Design

Fig. 7, 8, 9, 10, 12: Courtesy of the Simonds Family

Fig. 11: The Schlesinger Library, Radcliffe Institute, Harvard University, Photograph by Alan Golin Gass, 1951

Fig. 15: Photograph by Jen Saffron for Allegheny Commons Initiative

Fig. 18: Darlington Family Papers, 1753–1921, DAR.1925.01, Darlington Collection, Special Collections Department, University of Pittsburgh

Fig. 19: G. M. Hopkins, *Atlas of the Cities of Pittsburgh, Allegheny, and the Adjoining Boroughs*, 1872

Fig. 20: "The Golden Triangle" illustration is from *Twentieth-Century Pittsburgh, Volume One: Government, Business, and Environmental Change*, by Roy Lubove, © 1969. Reprinted by permission of the University of Pittsburgh Press.

Fig. 21: Smoke Control Lantern Slide Collection, University of Pittsburgh

Fig. 22: Courtesy the Mellon Family, Richard King Mellon Foundation

Fig. 23: W. Eugene Smith, American, 1918–1978, *Mayor David L. Lawrence*, 1955–1957, gelatin silver print, H: 10 1/2 in. x W: 12 15/16 in. (26.67 x 32.86 cm), Carnegie Museum of Art, Pittsburgh: Gift of the Carnegie Library of Pittsburgh, 82.32.349

Fig. 25: Margaret Bourke-White, © Getty Images

Fig. 26: Courtesy of the Western Pennsylvania Conservancy

Fig. 27: Courtesy of the *Pittsburgh Post-Gazette*, January 28, 1947

Fig. 33: Courtesy of Alcoa

Fig. 43: Gerald L. Brockhurst, British, 1890–1978, *Portrait of Sarah Mellon Scaife*, ca. 1940–1945, oil on canvas, H: 37 in x W: 30 1/2 in. (93.98 x 77.47 cm), Carnegie Museum of Art, Pittsburgh: Gift of Mr. and Mrs. Richard M. Scaife, 66.9.1

Fig. 46, 93: Courtesy of Charles Birnbaum and The Cultural Landscape Foundation

Figs. 51, 52: Courtesy of Matthews International

Fig. 54: From the collection of Reed Smith, LLC

Fig. 55, 58: John Ormsbee Simonds Collection, University of Florida George A. Smathers Libraries

Fig. 59, 80, 88, 92: The Pittsburgh Parks Conservancy and Heritage Landscapes, *Mellon Square Preservation, Interpretation & Management Plan*, 2009

Fig. 61: © Brady Stewart Studio Inc.

Fig. 65, 67, 68, 69, 70, 71: Courtesy of Pittsburgh History & Landmarks Foundation, *Whirlwind Walk: Architecture and Urban Spaces in Downtown Pittsburgh* (Pittsburgh: Pittsburgh History & Landmarks Foundation, 2011)

Fig. 66: Photograph by Colin Hines

Fig. 74: Courtesy of the *Pittsburgh Post-Gazette*, 1955

Fig. 75: Wonday Film Service, Inc.

Fig. 77: Photograph by Paul M. Penney for Wonday Film Service, Inc.

Fig. 82: Photograph by Ed Massery

Fig. 83, 85, 87, 90: Photograph by Melissa McMasters for The Pittsburgh Parks Conservancy

Fig. 84, 95, 96, 97, 98, 99, 100, 102, 103, 104, 105, 107: Photograph by John Altdorfer for The Pittsburgh Parks Conservancy

Fig. 86: Courtesy of Heritage Landscapes and The Pittsburgh Parks Conservancy

Fig. 89, 91, 101: Illustration by Heritage Landscapes for The Pittsburgh Parks Conservancy

Fig. 94: Illustration by Bob Bowden for The Pittsburgh Parks Conservancy

Fig. 106, 108: The Pittsburgh Parks Conservancy

Fig. 109, 112: Photograph by Edward F. Dumont for The Pittsburgh Parks Conservancy

Fig. 110: Photograph by Lauren Stalter for The Pittsburgh Parks Conservancy

Fig. 111: Courtesy of Heritage Landscapes and Pfaffmann & Associates